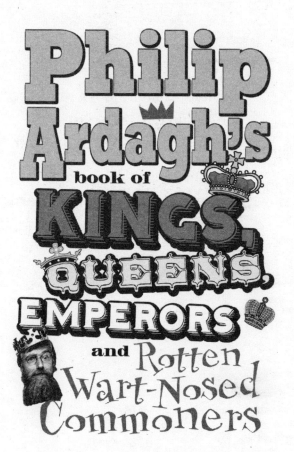

Philip Ardagh's book of KINGS, QUEENS, EMPERORS and Rotten Wart-Nosed Commoners

Also by Philip Ardagh

Philip Ardagh's Book of
Absolutely Useless Lists
for Absolutely Every Day of the Year

Philip Ardagh's Book of
Howlers, Blunders and Random Mistakery

Philip Ardagh's

book of

KINGS, QUEENS, EMPERORS

and Rotten Wart-Nosed Commoners

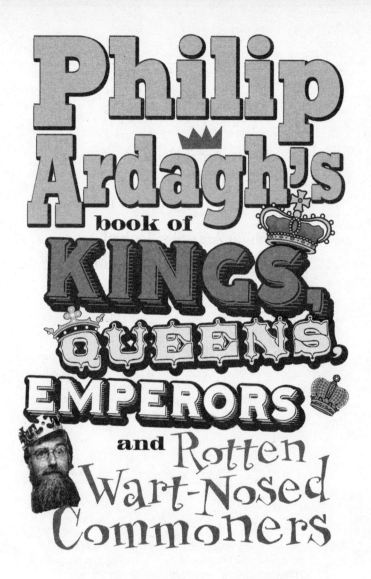

Illustrated by **Del Thorpe**

MACMILLAN

First published 2011 by Macmillan Children's Books
a division of Macmillan Publishers Limited
20 New Wharf Road, London N1 9RR
Basingstoke and Oxford
Associated companies throughout the world
www.panmacmillan.com

ISBN 978-0-330-47173-2

1 3 5 7 9 8 6 4 2

A CIP catalogue record for this book is available from
the British Library.

Printed and bound by CPI Group (UK) Ltd, Croydon CR0 4YY

A message from Philip Ardagh

Is everything in this book true? I doubt it.

But just about everything in this book is historical. The versions of events, though not always necessarily guaranteed one-hundred-per-cent-true-or-your-money-back factual, are ones that've been around a long time in their own right, often having passed into history themselves.

History, you see, ain't facts. History is the written version of our past which – hopefully – contains more truth than not. And history usually gets written by the victor. The army which wins the battle then tells the world how that battle was won (maybe exaggerating the size of the enemy forces and the bravery of its own commanders).

Here, then, are some of the more interesting titbits about a few of the very different folk who've peopled history along the way.

King of Grease!

One day in 1863, the Danish Prince William of Glücksberg (1845–1913) was unwrapping a sandwich for lunch when he discovered that he was now, at the age of seventeen, King of Greece. The sandwich – a sardine one, in case you were wondering – had been wrapped in a piece of old newspaper and – lo and behold! – there was an article announcing the news (a bit greasy in places from the fish oil).

When he moved into the palace in Athens, as King George I of Greece, he was impressed by the size of it. One of his favourite pastimes was to roller-skate around the ballroom! He was quick to learn Greek* and would often walk around the capital city, as informally as possible, which helped to make him a popular monarch with his people.

He was just two weeks short of ruling for an impressive fifty years when he was assassinated in March 1913.

---

* As well as Greek and his native Danish, William/ George also spoke German (mainly to his wife) and English (mainly to their eight children).

Lightning strikes twice

Edward I (1239–1307) was either an amazingly lucky or an amazingly *un*lucky monarch, depending on how you look at it. Take, for example, the time he was quietly playing a game of chess when a huge chunk of masonry came crashing down from the vaulted ceiling above. Unluckily for him, it landed where he was sitting. Luckily for him,

it was where he was sitting *moments before.* When the stone fell, he'd actually wandered away from the table.

Then there was the time he was out and about in Paris with his attendants and was almost struck by lightning. Almost. The lightning just missed him . . . and killed two of his attendants instead.

Edward had two nicknames. The first was Edward Longshanks because he was tall. He was 6 ft 2 in, which is still considered tall today but was *really* tall back then. He was an impressive, imposing figure and the Dean of St Paul's is said to have dropped dead at the sight of him!

His second nickname was the Hammer of the Scots, because of the wars he waged against his Scottish neighbours. He also wanted to keep the troublesome Welsh out of England, which is why so many Welsh castles – English-built but in Wales – were constructed during Edward's reign.

AUT VIAM INVENIAM AUT FACIAM*

Despite being King of England, George I (1660–1727) couldn't speak English. His native tongue was German. Britain's first prime minister, Sir Robert Walpole, couldn't speak German. *His* native tongue was English (with a Norfolk farmer's accent). French was the official language of diplomacy (spoken by ambassadors and the like), but George and Walpole managed to communicate by talking to each other in Latin. Thank heavens for a classical education!

* 'I will either find a way or make one.'

4

The *White Ship* Disaster

Henry I's life (c.1068–1135) was shattered when two of his sons – William and Richard – were drowned. They were among a number of noble passengers aboard a brand new vessel, *La Blanche-Nef.** It was owned by Thomas FitzStephen, whose father had been a captain of one of William the Conqueror's ships during the invasion of England back in 1066.

FitzStephen offered Henry the use of his ship for his return to England from France, but the king had already made arrangements, so suggested that his boys use it instead.

La Blanche-Nef set off in darkness and in next to no time hit a submerged rock and capsized with remarkable speed. The cause of the accident remains uncertain. There were many theories at the time, ranging from it being an act of God because the ship hadn't been properly blessed by priests before setting off on its maiden voyage, to the whole crew being drunk. (There was certainly a lot of wine on board.)

* *The White Ship.*

5

Despite there being many noblemen and noblewomen aboard, the only known survivor was a butcher from Rouen. He wasn't rescued from the cold seas by fishermen until the following morning, but had been saved from exposure by having worn thick ram skins.

A chronicler* has it that when Thomas FitzStephen struggled to the surface and realized that William had drowned, he decided to let himself drown too, rather than face Henry.

It is said that once the king did hear the news, he never smiled again.

* Orderic Vitalis.

Paws for thought

The President of Mexico – at the time when Texas* broke free from that country – was the dictator General López de Santa Anna (1794–1876). On 6 March 1836, at the Battle of the Alamo, Santa Anna's army killed between 187 and 250 Texan defenders,** later executing a further 350 Texan prisoners. The Battle of the Alamo went down in history as one of the greatest, bravest defeats.*** What's less remembered is that Santa Anna was a huge fan of the world's smallest breed of dog: the chihuahua (pronounced shee-wa-wa), named after Mexico's largest state. The general even had chihuahuas trotting around after him at the Alamo!

* Texas went from being a part of Mexico to an independent republic to one of the United States of America.
** Including Davy Crockett (with the funny hat) and James Bowie (after whom the bowie knife is named).
*** And the subject of a number of movies, probably the most famous being *The Alamo*, starring John Wayne.

Have a heart

Robert the Bruce of Scotland* (1274–1329) really put his heart into the Crusades. Not literally. He had someone (try to) do that for him. The Bruce died before he had a chance to travel to the Holy Land to fight the Saracens, but not before he'd had his brainwave. He gave instructions that once he'd died, Sir James Douglas** was to cut out his heart, embalm it and take it with him to the Holy Land . . . which Sir James did, or tried to. According to some versions of events, Sir James wore the heart in a silver casket around his neck. On the way to the Middle East, he fought against the Moors in Spain. When things seemed hopeless, Sir James chucked the casket at the oncoming enemy, shouting, 'Lead on, brave heart, I'll follow thee!' and charged after it. He was killed.

* Probably best remembered for his (fictitious) meeting with a spider.
** Also known as Sir James the Good, which wasn't a bad nickname.

In 1331, Sir James's body was returned to Scotland along with Robert the Bruce's heart, but people lost track of its whereabouts. In 1996, a lead container was found under the floor of the chapter house at Melrose Abbey in Scotland. It was taken to Edinburgh where it was opened to reveal *another* lead container on which a plaque read:

> The enclosed leaden casket
> containing a heart
> was found beneath
> Chapter House floor, March 1921,
> by His Majesty's Office of Works

It was decided *not* to open this second container. It was simply reburied at Melrose Abbey in 1998.

The symbol of the heart was added to the Douglas family coat of arms.*

* One of the most famous members of the Douglas family was the Marquess of Queensberry, who invented the Queensberry Rules of boxing.

Gone and best forgotten

Henry VIII had six wives – divorced, beheaded, died, divorced, beheaded, survived – the first of whom was Catherine of Aragon (1485–1536). She was a very popular queen and had a huge following, particularly with Catholics when Henry broke away from the Church of Rome to set up the Church of England. He divorced her.

When Catherine died in 1536, it took the king six weeks to have her buried. Ex-queens were unusual, so he wasn't sure what to do with her remains. By rights, she should probably have been buried in London at some grand ceremony, but by then, she was an embarrassment to him. Instead, he had her buried in the abbey church of Peterborough.*

Important people were buried near the high altar in churches, but not Catherine. Henry ordered that she be buried in the north-west transept as a deliberate insult to her memory.

* Which is, today, Peterborough Cathedral.

When the king was approached with the idea of building a large monument to his dead (first) wife, he famously replied that he 'would have raised to her memory one of the goodliest monuments in Christendom'. This caused much puzzlement when the only thing to mark her resting place was a plaque on the floor.

All became clear during the Dissolution of the Monasteries, when Henry VIII closed monasteries, priories, convents and friaries, claiming all their property and assets for the Crown.* Many buildings were destroyed (or their stone taken to build houses elsewhere). The abbey of Peterborough, however, was saved from this fate by royal decree: the fact that it still stands today is a monument to Catherine of Aragon.

* In other words, for *him*.

Chop, chop!

The Battle of Towton, fought on 29 March 1461, was without a doubt the bloodiest battle ever fought on English soil. Over 28,000 men were killed in the fighting on that single day . . . and both sides were fighting for the English because it was a civil war. The two armies were King Henry VI's Lancastrians and Edward of York's Yorkists.

By the time of the battle, Edward (1442–83) had already declared himself King Edward IV and, once his forces had soundly defeated Henry VI's, there were fewer people to argue with him . . .

King Henry (1421–71) himself had chosen not to take part in the Battle of Towton because 29 March that year was Palm Sunday, and he didn't think it was right to fight . . . though he didn't seemed to mind his *men* fighting and dying for him. These included (in alphabetical order) the Earls of Devonshire and Wiltshire. They survived the battle itself, but afterwards Edward of York – I mean King Edward IV, Your Majesty – had them beheaded.

As if brutal, non-stop hand-to-hand combat wasn't bad enough, the fighting that day took place in deep snow.

Make no bones about it

The church of St Mary of Charity* in Faversham, Kent, is reputed to be 'likely to contain' the remains of King Stephen (c.1092–1154) but there are many who dispute this. The reason? Because following the Dissolution of the Monasteries, there are clear reports of Stephen's tomb being destroyed at the abbey in Faversham, and his royal bones being unceremoniously thrown into the river.** But who's to say that they weren't fished out and reburied?

Or not.

* In the nineteenth century, the inside of the church was heavily restored and altered by Sir George Gilbert Scott, famous for designing St Pancras Station in London.
** Faversham Creek.

13

Like father, like son? Not a lot!

Henry II (1133–89) was said to have been *so* angered by the betrayal of his sons, particularly his eldest, Richard, that even his dead body had a nosebleed when the new king approached! Henry II was lying in state when blood started trickling from his nostrils 'as if his spirit was indignant at Richard's approach'.*

Richard had defeated his father in battle and, as the old king lay dying, he read him the names of his (Richard's) supporters so that Henry could officially pardon each of them – to avoid any divided loyalty from Henry's supporters following his death.

And the very first name at the top of the list? None other than Henry's youngest son, John.

His famous last words were: 'Shame, shame on a conquered king.'

* According to the chronicle of Benedict of Peterborough.

His heart wasn't in it

Richard the Lionheart's heart was not buried with the rest of him. Richard I (1157–99) – as he was also known – was buried in Fontevrault Abbey in France, which had been founded nearly a hundred years before his death. It was an unusual abbey because both monks and nuns lived there, when in most other abbeys it was either one or the other, not unisex!

For some reason, Richard wanted his heart to be buried in Rouen Cathedral, which it was. The heart was rediscovered in the nineteenth century, when it was put in a silver casket inside a lead box.

The Lionheart's heart was described as being, by that time, reduced to something like 'a dry, reddish leaf'.

Dear Queen

When Edward I (1239–1307) was still a prince, he married Eleanor of Castile, daughter of King Ferdinand III of Castile. (They ended up having sixteen children together.) Prince Edward took Eleanor with him to the Crusades, leaving Dover in 1270. In June 1272, an attempt was made to murder Prince Edward by a member of the secret society known as the Assassins. Having arranged to meet him on the pretext of talking secret business, the man drew a poisoned dagger and attacked Edward. A fight followed in which Edward actually managed to disarm the man. The prince was only wounded in the arm but unfortunately, coming from a poisoned dagger, the wound became infected. Eleanor nursed him back to health.

The two remained very close for the rest of their marriage. It was when she was accompanying her husband to Lincoln, in 1290, that Eleanor suffered the recurrence of a fever she'd had three years previously. By the time they reached the village of Harby in Nottinghamshire, she was too ill to go any further, dying in the home of one Richard de Weston.

Heartbroken, King Edward had a memorial cross put up at every spot where Eleanor's body was rested during its long journey back to London. The name Charing Cross* – as in Charing Cross Station, London – gets its name from one such cross. Today, a Victorian replica of the original cross stands in the station forecourt.

In Westminster, there is a fine tomb to Eleanor in St Edward's Chapel.

* Probably a corruption of *chère reine* (French for 'dear queen').

Anne's plan

Queen Anne (1665–1714) is remembered for being very dull and very overweight. She was known by her friend Sarah Churchill, the Duchess of Marlborough, as 'Mrs Freeman' and the queen, in turn, referred to her as 'Mrs Morley'. The reason? Anne was keen that they were able to talk to each other as equals, without formality, so they both dispensed with titles in private and called each other 'Mrs'!

Mrs Brown?

When her beloved husband Albert died, Queen Victoria (1819–1901) struck up a strong friendship with one of her Scottish servants, John Brown. Many members of the royal household disapproved of their behaviour and some referred to Victoria as 'Mrs Brown' behind her back.

In 2003, extracts were published of a diary written by Lewis Harcourt, son of Sir William Harcourt who was once home secretary in prime minister William Gladstone's government. In one entry, he wrote that the Rev. Norman McCloud* had confessed to his sister on his deathbed that he had married Queen Victoria to John Brown and had regretted it for the rest of his life. He concluded that Miss McCloud had nothing to gain from making up such a story, so he was inclined to believe it, 'improbable and disgraceful as it sounds'.

Most historians still think that such a marriage was highly unlikely, but we'll probably never know for sure.**

* The minister of Barony Church in Glasgow.
** Unless I can finish that time machine I'm building in the garage.

'Only kings, presidents, editors, and
people with tapeworms have the
right to use the editorial "we".'

Mark Twain

Bones on the move

Edward the Martyr (c.963–78) was King of England from 975 to 978, when he was murdered just outside Corfe Castle, probably on the orders of his stepmother. He was originally buried in nearby Wareham, but was moved to a more impressive tomb near the high altar in Shaftesbury Abbey when miracles were reported to have occurred at his original tomb, and he was declared a saint . . . but this wasn't his final resting place. His bones spent a number of years in a cutlery box* in the strongroom of a branch of the Midland Bank.** Edward's tomb in the abbey was revered and respected until the Dissolution of the Monasteries, when the whole building was stripped of all its valuables on the orders of King Henry VIII. Edward's bones had, however, been secretly removed and hidden elsewhere in the building.

* Designed for keeping knives, forks and spoons in it.
** Nowadays known as the HSBC.

In 1931, following an excavation led by John Wilson-Claridge, whose family now owned the site, a battered old casket was found. The remains inside were studied by experts and it was declared that the damage found on them was consistent with the injuries St Edward was reported to have received.

An argument then broke out between two members of the Wilson-Claridge family as to who owned the bones and where they should be laid to rest, and it was while this was being sorted out that they were left in the bank.

Two requirements made by Wilson-Claridge had to be met:

 that the bones be recognized as those of a saint

 that a shrine be created for them.

These conditions were agreed by the Russian Orthodox Church in Exile who placed Edward's remains in a shrine in a mortuary chapel in Brookwood Cemetery, near Woking in Surrey, in 1984.

A burning love

Richard II so loved his first wife, Anne of Bohemia (1366–94), that when she died of the plague at the palace of Sheen,* he ordered that the place be burned and anything that remained pulled down. Richard and Anne had been married in Westminster Abbey – which no other royalty did for another 537 years – and it was here that he had his own tomb built long before his death. As well as an effigy of himself on the tomb, there was also one of Anne next to his, holding hands with him. He is said to have visited it many times.

The entire route of Anne's funeral procession between St Paul's Cathedral and Westminster Abbey was lined with flaming torches and huge candles. When the Earl of Arundel arrived late, Richard was so angry that he hit him, causing him to fall on to the steps of the altar and cut his head, which bled badly!

* Originally a manor house near Richmond, enlarged and improved by Richard II who made it his main residence before Anne's death.

It seems that King Richard was a changed man when Anne died. Childless, and needing an heir, he got married again, this time to the seven-year-old Princess Isabella of France (creating a peace treaty between the two countries).

In 1399, Richard was overthrown by his cousin Henry Bolingbroke who became King Henry IV. He died, under suspicious circumstances, that same year.

Because I say so

Queen Victoria is famous for her love of her husband Prince Albert (1819–61), and her years of mourning – cutting herself off from the public – after his death. There are many constructions named after Albert, including: the Victoria and Albert Museum, the Albert Memorial in Kensington Gardens, London,* and the Albert Docks, Liverpool. Probably the most famous of all is the Royal Albert Hall, home to many performances including the annual BBC Proms, but it wasn't *supposed* to be called that.

Queen Victoria was invited to lay the foundation stone at a ceremony in 1871, where it was to be referred to as the Hall of Arts and Sciences . . . only Her Majesty went and called it the Royal Albert Hall of Arts and Sciences instead.

And that was the name they were stuck with.

* Also home to the famous statue of the fictional Peter Pan.

Witch stepmother?

Henry V didn't like his stepmother Joan of Navarre (1368–1437). In fact, he got it into his head that she was trying to kill him. Eventually, he either became convinced that she was a witch, or conveniently went along with the suggestion and used it to his advantage.

Either way, she was tried, found guilty (without a chance to defend herself), and had all her possessions – from clothes to money to property – seized. In 1419 she was imprisoned in Leeds Castle* and later in Pevensey Castle, East Sussex (originally a Roman fort, then a Saxon fortification and the first English castle used by William the Conqueror when invading in 1066).

After about four years, Henry V apparently had a change of heart – or attack of guilt – and set her free. Not only that, he gave her six dresses!**

* Which was – and still is – in the county of Kent, which is nowhere near Leeds in the county of Yorkshire.
** Well, at least that made up for the lost clothes, if not the lost money, property, land, and her imprisonment . . .

Fortunately for Joan, she lived the rest of her days in comfort in Nottingham Castle, and had an excellent relationship with Henry V's son, Henry VI.

When she died in 1437, she was buried in Canterbury Cathedral alongside her husband, Henry IV, in a splendid tomb.

'I name this ship *Me!*'

In September 1938, it seemed likely that Britain would go to war with Germany but, while gas masks were distributed and children evacuated, most aspects of life went on as usual. One such event was the official naming and launching of the Cunard ocean liner *Queen Elizabeth*.

It was King George VI's pleasant duty to name the ship after his wife and to release the bottle of champagne to smash against its hull, the signal for the ship's launch . . . except that he felt he was unable to attend. Britain's prime minister was in discussions with Adolf Hitler and the future of Britain was on a knife edge.

It was therefore King George's wife, Elizabeth* herself, who went to the Clydebank to launch the (then) world's largest ocean liner on 27 September . . . and to name it after herself.

Two days later, Chamberlain arrived by plane at Heston Aerodrome, waving a piece of paper and announcing 'Peace in our time!' He was wrong. A little under a year later, Britain was at war with Germany.

The *Queen Elizabeth*'s maiden voyage was as a troop carrier.

* Later Queen Elizabeth, the Queen Mother.

The naked wizard earl

Back in the days when James I of England (1566–1625) was just James VI of Scotland, he had more than a spot of bother with his cousin Francis Stewart, 5th Earl of Bothwell.

James VI was fond of Bothwell and even returned family lands to him which had been lost by his uncle, the 4th Earl (who'd been married to Mary, Queen of Scots, James's late mother).

Bothwell returned the favour by treating the Scottish king terribly. He tried kidnapping poor old James on numerous occasions, and behaved more and more erratically. Things came to a head when reports reached James that a conspiracy of witches in North Berwick had performed dark rites in an attempt to bring about his death . . . and that they had been led by 'the Wizard Earl of Bothwell'.

Bothwell was locked up in Edinburgh Castle while awaiting trial but managed to escape and, on 27 December 1591, ended up down the road outside James's bedroom door in Holyrood Palace.

Hearing a kerfuffle, King James threw open his door to find the wizard earl kneeling before him without a stitch of clothing on him, clutching a sword.

The king shouted 'Treason!', saying that he'd rather die than be taken prisoner and that Bothwell should do his worst. His bluff having been called, the somewhat confused wizard earl had no idea what to do next, so he surrendered.

From that day on, James VI is said to have been fearful for his own safety . . . and who could blame him? He went around wearing padded clothing in case of attack.

He got it in the end

Edmund II (c.988/993–1016), son of King Ethelred the Unready, gained the nickname 'Ironside' for putting up such a strong fight against the invading Danes, led by Canute. Finally, however, the two men shared the rule of England, dividing the kingdom (geographically) between them.*

Unfortunately for Ironside, he had the indignity of being murdered on the loo/lavatory/toilet or, to be more accurate, a privy: little more than a large poo-filled pit with a board across it for one to sit on.

Had Edmund had a genuine iron bottom rather than a metaphorical iron side, he might have survived the attack because a (very dedicated, very smelly) assassin lurked in the yucky pit below. Once the king was seated, the assassin struck with a dagger from beneath** and that was the – er – end of old Ironside!

* On Edmund's death, King Canute ruled the whole country.
** *Ouch!!!!*

31

The fall

In December 1918, just over a month after Armistice Day, when the First World War came to an end, King George V (1865–1936) visited British troops and graves in France, as well as touring the battlefields. This morale-boosting exercise was slightly spoilt by the fact that a rousing 'three cheers' from troops startled the king's horse, causing it to rear up and throw George to the ground. If that wasn't undignified and painful enough, the horse then landed on top of the king, breaking his pelvis.

Closer to home

Henry IV (1367–1413) was told by a soothsayer that he would die in Jerusalem, which wasn't as unlikely as it sounded because many European knights, noblemen and monarchs were fighting Crusades in the Holy Land. Rather than putting him off going, Henry was keen to join the Crusades, possibly believing that if he died for the Christian cause this might help redeem him from having seized the English throne from his cousin Richard II. He was under an enormous amount of strain and had contracted a terrible skin disease – which may have been anything from eczema to leprosy – supposedly on the very day that he had an archbishop put to death. It itched terribly.

While praying at the shrine of Edward the Confessor in Westminster Abbey, Henry was suddenly struck down with some kind of fit and was taken to a small room of the abbey. When he asked where he was, he was told that he was in the Jerusalem Chamber. He responded by saying, 'Praise be to the Father of Heaven, for now I know I shall die in the chamber, according to the prophecy of the aforesaid that I should die in Jerusalem.'

Legend has it that, as he lay dying, he was urged to repent of his two greatest sins: having seized the throne of England and having an archbishop executed. He is said to have replied that his sons would never forgive him giving up the crown, and that the Pope had already forgiven him for the archbishop's death anyway.

What's in a name?

The wife of George III (1738–1820) was Queen Charlotte, but there are some suggestions that he was secretly married to someone else already: Hannah Lightfoot, a Quaker. In fact, it's said that when he was still a prince, he married Hannah twice: firstly at a secret ceremony at Kew Chapel in April 1759, and then again in May – at an equally hush-hush Church of England service – in their own home. What *is* known is that they did have a relationship.

Things got really interesting when rumours grew up around a certain George Rex* who, it was claimed, was the eldest son of Hannah and George. If Hannah and George really were married, this would have made George Rex an heir to the English throne. According to this version of events, George and Hannah sent him to live in South Africa, never to return. Had George Rex really been the king's son and married and had children of his own, then his children, in turn, might have had legitimate claims to the throne . . .

---

* Latin for 'King'. It was probably the name which started the rumour in the first place.

In his will, Rex went out of his way to make it clear that he had never married the mother of his children. Was this because, to avoid such complications, George III had insisted that the boy promise not to marry?

The answer is a resounding 'No!' DNA tests on the descendants of George Rex show that he didn't have a drop of royal blood in him. But it does make a great story.

Dw i ddim yn deall!*

In recent history, the eldest son of the British monarch has regularly been given the title Prince of Wales. This isn't a title he's born to but one he's given by the king or queen. Prince Charles** (1948–) – the Prince of Wales at the time I'm writing this – is only the twenty-first Prince of Wales since the title was founded in 1301.

The current prince was given the title when he was nine years old but it wasn't until he was twenty that he attended his 'investiture' at Caernarvon Castle in Wales.***

Some Welsh people – particularly the Welsh Nationalists, who believe that Wales should be a separate country to England – were against the event on 1 July 1969, but it passed off peacefully.

* Means 'I don't understand.'
** Prince Charles, Prince of Wales, KG, KT, GCB, OM, AK, QSO, CD, SOM, GCL, PC, AdC(P), FRS.
*** A bit like a monarch coming to the throne but not being crowned until sometime later

37

Unusually – possibly uniquely – for a Prince of Wales, Prince Charles actually tried to get a basic grasp of the Welsh language and gave a speech in Welsh to the Welsh youth organization Urdd Gobaith Cymru just a few weeks before his investiture. (He took a crash course at the University of Wales in Aberystwyth.) It is unlikely that his father, the Duke of Edinburgh, actually speaks Scottish . . .

A not-so-secret mission

In 1623 two men calling themselves John
and Thomas Smith, and wearing obviously
false beards, arrived from England in Madrid,
Spain. Their mission? To try to win the heart
of Anna, a Spanish princess. One of these
'Smiths' went by the name 'Steenie'. This was
a nickname given to him by none other than
King James I himself, after St Stephen who
was said to have had 'the face of an angel'. He
was George Villiers, Duke of Buckingham. The
other so-called 'Smith' was heir to the English
throne: the future Charles I.*

Steenie ended up have a flaming row with
the English Ambassador in Spain, the Earl
of Bristol, and Charles's attempts to woo
Princess Anna failed when Charles refused
Spain's demands that, as part of the marriage
settlement, he should convert to Roman
Catholicism and stay in Spain for a year after
the wedding.

* Who ended up having his head chopped off.

Rather than coming home engaged, Charles and Steenie* returned wanting war with Spain.

Don't hang up!

As a child, King John (1167–1216) was engaged to Princess Alais of Savoy but she died before they could marry so, in 1189, he married Isabel, Countess of Gloucester (for money) instead. Then he met Isabelle of Angoulême (1188–1246) and fell head over heels in love, so he had his marriage annulled.

In 1200, John married twelve-year-old Isabelle. They went on to have five children together but, meanwhile, he also had twelve children with various different girlfriends. When he thought Isabelle had a boyfriend, though, he became enraged with jealousy. He not only had the man hanged by the neck until dead but also had his body hung above Isabelle's bed, as a warning to her.

Their marriage ended in 1216 when John died, either of dysentery or poisoned drink.

Royal pleasures

James I (1566–1625) is said to have introduced two sports to England:

1. Golf
2. Horse racing.*

James was Scottish (being King James VI of Scotland before also gaining the English crown), and Scotland is the home of golf. It was originally played on the coast, using pebbles instead of balls, and sand dunes as the bunkers.**

As for horse racing, the first recorded race was in 1604, when competitors had to ride five times between London and York from a Monday morning to the following Sunday night. It was won by one of James's grooms, who completed it on the Friday.

Horse races were held in Enfield and Croydon and were called 'bell courses' because the winner was given a silver bell (rather than the cup or cash prizes given today).

* Called 'horse running' at the time.
** Or, more to the point, the sand-filled bunkers on a golf course came to represent the sand dunes.

A cool plan

The Emperor Nero (AD 37–68) had his half-brother, Britannicus, murdered. He decided to poison him, but there was one teeny-weeny problem: Britannicus had a food taster whose job it was to taste his food and drink before he did, just to be sure that it *wasn't* poisoned. At Britannicus' last, fateful, meal his food taster sipped every drink and nibbled every dish before his master, as usual.

When the taster sipped some hot wine, found it was fine and handed it Britannicus, the Emperor's half-brother took a sip and found it far too hot. Some water was quickly added to cool it down, so now he could drink it with ease. There was only one problem, though. Britannicus hadn't had the cold water tasted. It had been poisoned and it killed him.

Sneaky old Nero.

'Parp!'

Pssst! Do you know the story about Queen Elizabeth I (1533–1603) and the – er – farting courtier? One day, when bowing low to Her Majesty, the Earl of Oxford couldn't help but break wind.

The poor man felt *so* embarrassed that he left the court – and some say the *country* – for *seven* years.

Upon his return, after such a long absence, the first thing Good Queen Bess said on seeing him was, 'Lord, I had forgot the fart!'

Pocillovist* alert!

Egg cups have been around for thousands of years and the first ones were most likely to have been made from wood. Today they come in everything from plastic to porcelain to silver.

King Louis XV of France (1710–74) was a big fan of egg cups and this led to their widespread popularity. He ate a boiled egg in an egg cup every Sunday, causing a craze for egg cups in eighteenth-century France.

He was said to be able to chop the top off his egg with a single stroke.

Just ninteen years after his death, it was the King of France** having his head chopped off.

* An egg cup collector, from the Latin *pocillum* = a small cup, and *ovi* = egg.
** Louis XVI.

Fiendish fish dish

The Japanese Emperor Akihito (1933–) is a world expert on goby fish, having had thirty-eight scientific papers on the subject published. It was Akihito, as crown prince, who introduced the bluegill fish from the United States in the 1960s, hoping that the fish would become a new source of food for his country. It became known as 'the prince of fish'.

Unfortunately, the bluegill started eating all the native fish instead!

In November 2007, the emperor publicly expressed regret at having brought the fish to Japan, causing the country's own fish stock to plummet. As a result of these comments, the central province of Shiga introduced a 'catch-and-eat' programme in Japan's largest lake, Lake Biwa, and even went so far as to publish a tasty bluegill sweet-and-sour recipe on their official government website.

A king, a bathroom and *La Joconde**

The world's most famous painting is perhaps the *Mona Lisa*, visited by over 8 million people a year. The painting, which was completed in 1507, is in the Louvre museum in Paris, where it's protected by 3 inches of bulletproof glass and a complicated alarm system . . . but it wasn't always quite so well looked after. In 1911, it was stolen by someone who'd hidden in a broom cupboard overnight, and then walked out with it under his coat when the museum opened the next day. (It was recovered in 1913.) Hundreds of years before that, though, this priceless masterpiece hung in a steamy bathroom.

The *Mona Lisa* was painted by Leonardo da Vinci, and King Francis I of France (1494–1547) persuaded him to spend what turned out to be the last three years of his life in his country. And it was in King Francis's bathroom that the painting hung for a while but – fortunately for the *Mona Lisa* – he had it moved to another room.

* The French name for the painting also known as the *Mona Lisa*.

Legend – which can have a habit of becoming history – has it that Leonardo actually died in the king's arms, in 1519. They had certainly become close friends. Twenty years later, King Francis is reported as having said, 'There had never been another man born in the world who knew as much as Leonardo, not so much about painting, sculpture and architecture, as that he was a very great philosopher.'

A flaming great idea!

Alfred the Great (AD 849–99) is well known for burning some cakes he was supposed to be keeping an eye on as a boy, but he still turned out great (even if the cakes didn't).

What's less well remembered – or basically forgotten – is that he is also credited with having invented the candle clock, where a candle has equally spaced markings, representing a particular burning time between each. Alfred's clock was made up of six candles, each divided into twelve sections and taking four hours to burn, giving a total of twenty-four hours.*

When Alfred first tried it outside, the flames kept blowing out . . . so he came up with the idea of protecting the flames in a lantern. Great result!

NEW! FROM ALFRED INC.

The CANDLE CLOCK

* Which means the marking must have been spaced twenty minutes' burning-time apart.

'It's nothing! It's nothing!'

The spark that started the First World War – or which certainly brought things to a head – is said to be the shooting dead of Archduke Franz Ferdinand of Austria on 28 June 1914.

He and his wife, Sophie, were in the third (open-top) car in a motorcade of six on an official visit to Sarajevo. One car was blown up by a bomb thrown by an anarchist, but, amazingly, the official tour continued. When Franz Ferdinand arrived at the town hall, he interrupted the mayor's opening speech, saying: 'Mr. Mayor, I came here on a visit and I get bombs thrown at me. It is outrageous.' At the end of the opening ceremony, though, he thanked the people of Sarajevo for their claps and cheers 'as I see in them an expression of their joy at the failure of the attempt at assassination.'

This over, the Archduke then decided that they should go to the hospital to visit those wounded in the bombing. Soon after taking a wrong turn, Franz Ferdinand and Sophie were shot. Just two bullets were fired, one hitting each of them. As his wife sat dying next to him in the back seat of the car, Franz cried out, 'Sophie! Don't die! Don't die! Live for the children!' Then, to reassure either himself or Sophie, he said, 'It's nothing!' six or seven times.

Sophie died before they reached the Governor's mansion to which their car was now speeding. Ferdinand died on a chaise longue within ten minutes of their arrival. For some strange reason, he had been sewn into his uniform that day.

Basket case?

Like so many other kings of France before and after him, Henry III of France (1551–89) was poodle mad! When out and about in the streets of Paris, he carried his favourites – Liline, Titi and Mimi – in a basket which he had 'slung around his neck'. (It's a shame no one ever drew a picture of this from life.)

These were the same poodles who barked a warning when Henry was attacked by a crazed monk, Jacques Clément, in 1589. Clément asked to see the king in private, then pulled a dagger out from under his cloak (or habit) and stabbed the dog-loving monarch.

It was too late for poor Henry, but the frantic barking did attract the king's attendants, who burst in and killed Clément. Henry died the next day, no doubt with his beloved poodles at his bedside.

Flaming likely!

In January 1393, King Charles VI of France (1368–1422) held a lavish party to celebrate the marriage of one of his wife Queen Isabeau of Bavaria's ladies-in-waiting. A Norman squire by the name of Huguet de Guisay somehow convinced the king that it would be a fun idea for His Majesty and various lords to dress up as wild men, chain themselves to each other and dance around the room.

They wore 'costumes of linen cloth sewn on to their bodies and soaked in resinous wax or pitch to hold a covering of frazzled hemp, so that they appeared shaggy & hairy from head to foot'.

The room was lit by torch-bearers and – at the suggestion of one of his fellow 'wild men' – Charles commanded that they stand at the side of the room and stay there because of the fire hazard. Unfortunately, when the Duke of Orléans turned up late, one of the first things he did was to grab a lighted torch and hold it up in front of the dancing weirdos, possibly to see if he could recognize who was under those shaggy disguises . . . but actually ended up setting them on fire!

One of the revellers, enjoying the entertainment, was the quick-thinking Duchess of Berry, who threw the end of her gown over one of the dancers to smother any flames, only to discover that it was the king himself she'd saved. Four of the wild men were killed. One saved himself by jumping in a tub full of water used for dishwashing.

There is a theory that none of this was an accident at all – that Huguet de Guisay had tricked the king into wearing such a flammable costume in the first place and arranged for the Duke of Orléans to arrive later and deliberately set fire to His Majesty.

But why?

Because King Charles VI was mad – can you think of any other reason why he'd have agreed to dress as a hairy wild man and leap about? – and Orléans was his brother. Perhaps they wanted a *new* king on the French throne?

Brotherly love

One day when Charles II (1630–85) was out walking, he had just two lords with him. Moments later, his brother James, Duke of York, came clattering past in a carriage protected by a whole host of guards. The Duke ordered his driver to stop and, leaning out of the carriage window, asked the king whether he thought it was safe for him to be wandering about in public with so little protection.

The king looked his younger brother in the eye. 'No danger,' he said, 'for no man would take away my life to make *you* king of England.'

Damned if you do . . .

The 1932 MGM film *Rasputin and the Empress* was based on true events surrounding the murder of the 'mad monk' Rasputin in pre-communist Russia. One of those who killed Rasputin was a Prince Yusupov who was still alive and well when the film was being made . . . so the producers thought it best to change the name of the character played by movie star John Barrymore to 'Prince Chegodieff', to avoid the risk of being sued for defamation of character.

This sensible precaution backfired in a triple whammy.

Firstly, Yusupov sued MGM for *not* showing his true role in the murder, and they ended up paying him a huge amount of damages. Then there was the matter of his wife, whose character appeared under the name Princess Natasha but was clearly identifiable. She sued and won too. (They even had to cut certain scenes from the movie.)

Which leaves the small matter of the person who *really* went by the name of Prince Chegodieff, the supposedly 'fictional' name they'd given the Yusupov character, and who'd had nothing to do with Rasputin's death. He wasn't happy at a character bearing his name being portrayed as a murderer, so they ended up paying *him* damages too!

Too offal to think about

At his home in Nuneham Courtenay near Oxford, the then Archbishop of York, Lord Harcourt, had a number of strange possessions but none more so than the embalmed heart of King Louis XIV of France who'd died over a hundred years before, in 1715. Harcourt had bought the heart from grave-robbers who'd stolen it from the king's tomb during the French Revolution.

One day, the Archbishop had a visit from the Dean of Westminster, Dr William Buckland, who'd made it his life's ambition to eat as many different kinds of animal as possible. He'd eaten everything from toasted mice to

crocodiles and took the whole thing very seriously. He regularly went to London Zoo to get his hands on any recently deceased animal . . . to take home to cook.

When Dr Buckland laid eyes on the heart he only had one thought in mind: eating it. Which he did, saying: 'I have eaten many strange things in my lifetime, but never before have I eaten the heart of a king.'

England's most-married monarchs

Most people seem to know that England's most married king was Henry VIII (1491–1547), who had six wives. What few people seem to be aware of is that Henry's sixth and final wife, Catherine Parr (1512–48), was England's most married queen.

Before she was married to Henry VIII, she was married, in turn, to Edward Borough and John Neville. After her marriage to Henry ended with his death, she married her fourth and final husband, Thomas Seymour.

There is some confusion as to which Edward Borough Catherine was actually married to. For a long time, it was thought to be the 2nd Baron Borough of Gainsborough, but nowadays it's commonly accepted that she was actually married to that particular Edward Borough's grandson, who shared the same name. He died. There's no confusion as to who John Neville was: he was the 3rd Baron Latimer, of Snape Castle. He died too.

After her marriage to Henry VIII, and *his* death, Catherine married Thomas Seymour, the brother of Henry's third wife, Jane Seymour. He was the only one of Catherine's four husbands to outlive her.

Horsing about

Many royals from many countries over many centuries have been killed after falling from their horses. These include:

Fulk of Jerusalem falling from his horse while out hunting in 1143. He would probably have been fine if his heavy wooden saddle hadn't promptly fallen off after him, striking him on the head. He died of the resulting injuries.

Henry II's son Geoffrey, Duke of Brittany, being trampled to death by his horse during a tournament in 1186.

Frederick I of Barbarossa dying as he attempted to cross the Saleph River in Cilicia in 1190. The fall from his horse didn't kill him, but apparently the shock of landing in the cold water did. It gave him a heart attack, and *that's* what killed him.

Enguerrand III, Lord of Coucy, dying when he fell from his horse in 1242 . . . directly on to his own sword. (Ouch!)

King Alexander III of Scotland dying when his horse went off the road in the dark, in 1286, carrying him over a cliff . . .

Marjorie Bruce, daughter of Robert the Bruce, falling from her horse in 1316, causing her to go into premature labour. She gave birth to her son Robert Stuart, before dying a few hours later. The boy grew up to become King Robert II of Scotland, the first Stuart king.

William III of England dying as a result of injuries sustained from falling off his horse in 1702, after it tripped on a molehill!

'My children are not royal; they just happen
to have the Queen for their aunt.'

Princess Margaret
sister of Queen Elizabeth II

Feeling horrid, Henry?

Today, we often think of Henry VIII (1491–1547) as always being rather a plump king of England. There was, however, a time when he was young, dashing and much, much, slimmer. But he was accident-prone, and good at getting ill too.

- In 1514, he caught smallpox (which can be a killer).

- In 1521, he caught malaria from a mosquito bite (which was another potential killer).

- In 1524, he left his visor up and open during a friendly joust and ended up with a broken lance in his face. (There were fears for his life.)

- In 1525, he tried pole-vaulting a ditch. The pole snapped and Henry landed in the mud with such force that his head got stuck and he found it difficult to breathe.

- In 1528, he started developing ulcers on his legs, which got worse and worse over time, making it hard for him to walk.

- He was also a lifelong sufferer of really bad headaches.

Apart from these – and maybe one or two other things – he was as fit as a fiddle!

Keeping it in the family

Spain was ruled by the Hapsburgs for nearly two hundred years, starting with King Charles I in 1516 and ending in 1700 when Hapsburg King Charles II died without any heirs. Other branches of the Hapsburgs ruled Austria for over 600 years.

In order to make sure that Spain stayed in the Spanish Hapsburg family, most Spanish Hapsburgs married other Spanish Hapsburgs. Of the eleven royal marriages in the 200-year period, nine were between very close relatives. Such 'inbreeding' is not good for the genetic make-up of families, often leading to ever-increasing genetic weaknesses.

In 2009, Gonzalo Alvarez and his colleagues at the University of Santiago de Compostela in Spain released a study – based on genealogical information for Charles II and 3,000 of his relatives and ancestors – showing the calculated effect of such close intermarrying for each individual across sixteen generations of the Habsburgs.

They concluded that King Charles's inability to have children and various other defects – his nickname was 'The Hexed', suggesting he was jinxed – were based on two specific genetic disorders, brought about by Hapsburg repeatedly marrying Hapsburg.

On the up and up

The mother of Anne Hyde, James II's wife, was a 'tub-woman' (or so the story goes). It was her job to carry great big tubs of beer from a brewery, until the brewer took a fancy to her and married her, conveniently dying soon after and leaving her a significant fortune. (There was big money in beer-making.) The widow sought advice from an up-and-coming lawyer as to the best way to manage her newly found wealth. His suggestion was that she should marry him! It was a well-made match. He started out as plain Mr Hyde – Anne was their daughter – but he ended up the Earl of Clarendon and became Lord Chancellor.

Although Anne died before James (1633– 1801) ever became king,* two of her children did get to wear the crown in their own right as Queen Mary II and Queen Anne, the last of the Stuart monarchs.

* He married again on her death.

Look, no hands!

There were many spectacular entertainments and wonderments arranged to mark the coronation of Henry VIII's son, nine-year-old Edward VI (1537–53), in 1547, but one of the stranger ones involved the 520-foot spire of St Paul's Cathedral.* A rope was fixed to the top of it, reaching all the way down to the ground by the Deanery, and it was down this that a Spanish acrobat slid – yes, *slid* – on his chest – yes, chest.

Now *that's* what I call entertainment, and the young king would certainly have agreed with me. He actually stopped to watch, having his feet kissed by the acrobat who then – *wait for it . . . wait for it* – shinned all the way up the rope to the top of the spire again!

* This was of course what we now think of as *old* St Paul's Cathedral – because the current one doesn't even have a spire but a dome – but, in those days, it was simply St Paul's (because there wasn't a new one to compare it with).

Interestingly, the acrobat – whose name seems not to be recorded anywhere – was from Aragon, in Spain. This was where Henry VIII's first wife, Catherine,* had come from; the wife whom he'd divorced so that he could marry Anne Boleyn whom he then beheaded – enabling him to marry Jane Seymour (who later gave birth to Edward).

It's a small (cruel) world!

* Of Aragon!

Gone and best forgotten?

After the death of her beloved husband, Prince Albert, Queen Victoria (1819–1901) became a recluse, steering clear of appearing in public if humanly possible. Meanwhile her eldest son, Edward, Prince of Wales, was very much in the public eye but behaving scurrilously.

With the queen so much in the background, anti-royalist feelings were more and more vocalized, with many people openly talking about the monarchy being swept away and replaced with a republic.

The prime minister, William Gladstone, himself pointed out that 'the Queen is invisible and the Prince of Wales is not respected'.

Anti-Victoria pamphlets were published and widely distributed, including the likes of 'Mrs John Brown' (referring to her close relationship with her Scottish servant, John Brown).

Things looked very bad for Queen Victoria in particular and the British monarchy in general.

Then the Prince of Wales caught typhoid and it looked as though he might die. Not only that, it seemed that he might die exactly ten years to the day after his father, Albert, had died. In many people's minds, this pulled into focus the very human element of the tragedy: a widow about to lose a son.

While the queen sat at her son's bedside, waiting for the worst, much of the nation seemed to be waiting too. Bell-ringers were on standby at St Paul's Cathedral ready to sound the death knell – ring the bells – to mark His Royal Highness's passing . . .

. . . but, somehow, Edward pulled through.

On 27 February 1872, Queen Victoria attended St Paul's Cathedral for a special service of thanksgiving for her son's recovery. The streets were lined with thousands of cheering people.

Such was the euphoria and enthusiasm from people seeing Victoria in public that she even went out on to the balcony of Buckingham Palace to acknowledge the throng of people surging into the Mall.

Calls for republicanism were dead. The queen was back.

Feathers fly

The Emperor Honorius (384–423) was a big fan of birds, keeping pigeons and chickens. He loved chickens. According to Procopius of Caesarea* in his book *The Vandalic War*, his favourite bird was a cockerel he'd named Rome.

Procopius writes of an occasion when the emperor was in Ravenna when news reached the household that the city of Rome had been taken over by Alaric's army of Goths. One of his servants told him 'that Rome had perished. And he cried out and said, "And yet it has just eaten from my hands!"' Honorius had thought he'd been talking about his beloved bird. The servant then 'explained that it was [not the bird but] the city of Rome which had perished at the hands of Alaric,' causing the emperor to give 'a sigh of relief'.

Most historians seem to think that the story was made up, but it does reflect what the public probably thought of the emperor at the time!

* Secretary to the Roman general Belisarius.

Playing chicken

The Emperor Napoleon of France (1769–1821) was a man who liked to be prepared. Just in case he got hungry at night, he went through a period of ordering his servants to have a ready-roasted chicken on standby every night.

Of course, none would dare disobey him – so a fresh chicken was duly roasted every evening – but then again, most nights Napoleon *didn't* wake up demanding a whole chicken so, on some occasions, the servants would nibble a bit here and there.

Unfortunately, on one occasion when Napoleon did wake up, and did feel peckish, and did ask for his chicken . . . the chicken he was served up was a little *incomplete*.

The emperor asked since when there had been one-legged one-winged chickens running about the place, and he ended up pulling the ears of the servants who'd eaten them.

75

Seeds of doubt

In 1887, Louise Cresswell wrote a book entitled *Eighteen Years on the Sandringham Estate* under the pseudonym 'The Lady Farmer'. The Sandringham estate was home to Queen Victoria and Prince Albert's son, the future King Edward VII (1841–1910), and Cresswell had been one of his tenant farmers* until seven years previously.

Edward ordered every copy be bought and burned. Why? Because 'The Lady Farmer' was far from complimentary about certain aspects of life on the estate!

Sandringham, for example, had one of the largest – if not *the* largest – larders in the world. This was to accommodate the 30,000 or so game birds shot on his estate each year . . . birds which themselves needed feeding and which, according to the book, ended up eating other people's crops in surrounding areas, much to the annoyance of the farmers. Such an accusation really rubbed His Royal Highness up the wrong way!

* At Appleton Farm.

Mrs Cresswell also had a number of personal disputes with Edward (then Prince of Wales) and with the prince's local agent, Mr Edmund Beck; some petty, some more serious.

Despite the pseudonym, it was abundantly clear to Edward who 'The Lady Farmer' was, and he didn't want people reading her version of her life in his shadow.

Action replay of the ghostly kind

Only once has an English royal commission officially accepted the existence of ghosts and – mass fraud and mass hallucination aside – it's difficult to see what other conclusion they could have come to!

In October 1642, Royalist forces led by King Charles II himself fought the Roundhead army led by the Earl of Essex at the Battle of Edgehill, near Stratford-upon-Avon. Over 1,000 soldiers – around 500 on either side – were killed.

Now comes the weird part. Three days later, a group of shepherds claimed to have seen the whole battle being re-fought right in front of them, but this time by ghosts. As if that weren't unlikely enough, during the following weeks, many, many – *many*, get that? – people claimed to have witnessed the battle being re-fought by ghosts on a number of separate occasions.

Soon sightseers were turning up by the hundred, specifically in the hope of seeing something, and many claimed that they did.

In January the following year, a report on these extraordinary events appeared in print. This now had Charles's full attention. He sent the royal commission, and they reported having seen the ghostly battle not once but twice in two days.

Strangest of all, these royal officials not only swore on oath to having heard the terrible sounds of battle and witnessed it being played out before them by ghostly figures, but also said that they could actually identify many of these ghosts as particular people – friends and comrades – who'd died at the Battle of Edgehill.

Explain that!

Heading for a fall

Cardinal Thomas Wolsey (c.1471–1530) was one of Henry VIII's Lord Chancellors, which was really the top job. Over time, the power seemed to go to Wolsey's head. When he started out in the role, the cardinal used to issue orders by saying, 'The king says . . .' As he got more comfortable in his job, he started saying, 'We say . . .' Over time, he dropped mention of Henry altogether, and simply issued his orders with an 'I say . . .'

This was a rather dangerous thing to do.

Thomas Wolsey was the son of a butcher, so his rise to power was all the more impressive. He loved expensive possessions and liked to wear fancy clothes. (Speaking of fancy, he rather fancied the idea of being Pope one day, too.) He always appeared in public dressed in red. He was a particular fan of crimson or scarlet. It showed off his gold chain of office so nicely.

Wolsey was also fabulously rich. (There were rumours flying about that he'd used some of the royal treasury funds to boost his own.) He used to own a fabulous house called Hampton Court but – as so often happened if Henry VIII stayed in a place and decided he liked it – the king 'persuaded' him to give it to him as a present, so it became a royal palace!

Being a cardinal* as well as Lord Chancellor, he was given the job of finding a way of getting Henry out of his first marriage (so that he could marry again) which would satisfy the Pope and the Catholic Church. This was an impossible task, and Henry blamed Wolsey when it all went wrong.

Soon the cardinal found other people occupying his room at court. He found the king 'busy' when he wanted to speak to him. Finally, he was told to surrender his seal of office.** He refused until he was shown the king's own handwriting on the orders. When he recognized it, he's said to have broken down in tears.

* One of a group of a hundred or so Catholic bishops in the Sacred College, who advised the Pope.
** The Lord Chancellor's great seal was a symbol of his power and authority. Handing it in is like a cop handing in his badge or shield.

Henry VIII is probably best remembered for three things: his six wives, breaking away from the Catholic Church,* and his love of having people's heads chopped off . . . and he certainly wanted Thomas Wolsey to lose his. There would need to be some kind of trial first, of course, but everyone knew what the outcome would be: off with his head.

But King Henry didn't get his way this time. Wolsey died before he even went to trial.

He's supposed to have said that if he'd served God as well as he'd served his king, God wouldn't have given him grey hairs.

* Which included the Dissolution of the Monasteries.

Lance? No chance!

In 1559, King Henri II of France (1519–59) was enjoying a day on the jousting field and decided to round it off by challenging the Count of Montgomery to one last joust. His wife, Queen Catherine de' Medici, was against the idea. She'd had not one but *two* premonitions that such a contest would end in disaster, and pleaded with Henri not to fight, but he wouldn't listen.

Queen Catherine then turned her attention to the count, trying to persuade him to refuse to fight. Without him to joust against, the king would have to call the whole thing off. To Catherine's relief, Montgomery agreed and told the king there'd be no contest . . .

. . . which would have been fine if Henri hadn't been king and Montgomery a captain in his Scots Guards, but he *was* king, so he simple *ordered* Montgomery to be his opponent, and the count dared not refuse!

The joust went ahead and Montgomery's lance shattered, sending one enormous splinter through the king's eye, and another deep into his throat. Ten days later, Henri died.

83

Dead bored

When the 4th Earl of Huntly was tried in the Scottish courts and found guilty of treason, in 1562, he couldn't care less. He didn't bat an eyelid when the sentence of death was passed either – or, come to that, when he was beheaded. The reason was simple enough: he was already dead. It was his embalmed corpse that was receiving all this treatment.

His fellow accused, Sir John Gordon, was less fortunate, though. One of the Earl's twelve sons, Sir John didn't have the advantage of having died of natural causes before the trial. He was very much alive when it came to the execution, which was a badly botched job. Mary, Queen of Scots (1542–87), who had been the intended target of Huntly and Gordon's kidnap plot, broke down in tears as she witnessed the bungled hacking at his neck.

Escape or death?

According to the history books, after being forced to abdicate, King Edward II was horribly murdered in Berkeley Castle in 1327, where he was being kept prisoner. But one man claimed that it wasn't Edward's body that ended up being buried in the splendid tomb in Gloucester Cathedral.

In 1878, a letter written by a priest at Avignon in France to Edward's son, Edward III, was discovered. The letter, written in 1337, became known as the 'Fieschi Letter' after its author, Manuele Fieschi, who claimed that Edward II did not die.

According to Fieschi, Edward got wind of the plan to murder him. He managed to escape by changing clothes with a loyal manservant and, in this disguise, reached the castle gatehouse where he overpowered and killed the gatekeeper (or 'porter'). He then made good his escape.

When the knights arrived with murder on their mind, they found their royal victim gone, but – so Fieschi claimed – were too nervous to return to their mistress* with news of failure. They cut the heart from the dead gatehouse keeper and sent that to the queen, claiming it to be Edward's. As for the body in the tomb? It may well have been that of the gatekeeper too.

As for Edward, the priest claimed that he lived a hermit's life somewhere in continental Europe, trying to atone for his sins.

No one seems to think that the letter is a forgery. What is questioned is whether what Fieschi wrote – some ten years after the events he described – is the truth.

---

* It was Edward's own wife, Queen Isabella, who apparently ordered his death.

Maid of stern stuff

Henry VIII (1491–1547) divorced his first wife, Catherine of Aragon – which involved a split with the Pope and the Catholic Church – and married Anne Boleyn. Many key figures in the Church abroad strongly disapproved of his actions, but there was not a lot the king could do about that. At home was a different matter. (He ended up dissolving the monasteries: closing the buildings, stealing their riches for himself, and throwing out the monks.) But some of his critics made him nervous.

One such person was the Holy Maid of Kent, who began life as a servant girl but became a nun. Elizabeth Barton had spoken out against the divorce, but was even more critical now that the king had remarried. She predicted that God would exact his revenge, and that Henry would either be overthrown by God, or those acting for Him, within a month.

Two questions instantly spring to mind. Firstly, why should anyone believe a word this woman said? Secondly, why didn't Henry have her head chopped off there and then?

The reason why Elizabeth 'Holy Maid of Kent' Barton had such a following was threefold: she had been cured of what was considered an incurable disease, some of her previous predictions had come to pass, and – even more importantly – she carried a 'golden letter' which she claimed had been sent down from Heaven by God Himself . . . and you couldn't have much more authority than *that*.

Barton would often seem to go into impressive trances, sometimes for days at a time, and reported visions she had of the Virgin Mary. In some quarters, she was far more popular than the king so, for the time being, he left her well alone.

Before having her arrested, Henry made sure that her reputation was tainted. Rumours were spread about her being mentally ill or her behaving in a very un-nunlike fashion. Only *then* did he have her arrested, along with a handful of her closest supporters, and forced her to publicly declare that the whole thing was a hoax. They were then thrown in the Tower of London.

But Henry was wise enough to realize that there'd always be those who thought she'd only admitted the hoax under torture, when people were inclined to say anything. So he waited . . .

He waited until the Holy Maid of Kent was no longer news. Then, when most people had forgotten all about her, he had her hanged. As for Anne Boleyn, his second wife, he soon grew tired of her too. He had her head chopped off.

In other words

In September 2010, a new rug was installed in the Oval Office at the White House, the official residence of the President of the United States. The rug had a number of quotes woven into the fabric, including a favourite of President Barack Obama (1961–), the USA's first black president. Attributed not to a king but to a man named King – Martin Luther King Jr* (1929–68), the black civil rights activist – it read: 'The arc of the moral universe is long, but it bends toward justice.'

What President Obama didn't realize, and the rug makers didn't realize and a whole host of other people didn't realize was that, although King did, indeed, often use these words, he was himself quoting someone else: the 19th century abolitionist** Theodore Parker . . . a fact that is even mentioned in Wikipedia!

* He was assassinated/murdered.
** One who wanted to abolish the slave trade in black people.

All three not Dimitry

Dimitry I of Russia ruled for just ten months (from July 1605 to May 1606), after which he was shot, having jumped from a window and broken his leg, when fleeing plotters. His body was cremated and the ashes then fired from a cannon in the direction of Poland.

Why?

Perhaps because, although he'd *claimed* to be Dimitry, the youngest son of Ivan the Terrible, it was generally accepted that he was an impostor, and some thought him the illegitimate son of the King of Poland. Whoever he was, it's extremely unlikely he was Dimitry – records suggest the lad was murdered when he was nine – which is why he's commonly remembered as 'False Dimitry I'.

Then along came False Dimitry II, claiming that *he* was the genuine article. Despite the 'II' after his name, he never ruled as Tsar. It's simply a way of telling him apart from False Dimitry I. This impostor did manage to gain a fair amount of support, however, including an army of 100,000 soldiers, ready to take Moscow by force . . . but, as opposition grew, most of these men deserted. False Dimitry II ended up being killed in 1610 when drunk.

The third Dimitry, now known as – you guessed it – False Dimitry III, also went by the nickname of the Thief of Pskov. He was more of a tsar than False Dimitry II – who never was, remember – but less of a tsar than Dimitry I because, although he managed to get the Cossacks to acknowledge him as such in March 1612, few others accepted him and, by May that same year, the Moscow authorities had captured and killed him.

And that was the last of the Dimitry pretenders.

'In a few years there will be only five kings in the world: the King of England and the four kings in a pack of cards.'

King Farouk of Egypt

This unholy day

The 14th of December was not a happy date in Queen Victoria's household. Her husband, Prince Albert, died on that day in 1861. By a cruel twist of fate it was seventeen years later *to the day* that Victoria's second daughter, Alice* – who'd been present at Albert's death – also died. Aged thirty-five, she was the first of Her Majesty's children to die.

The jinx of 14 December was broken in 1895 when her great-grandson, the future king George VI (father of Queen Elizabeth II), was born. He never expected to be king, but was on the British throne during the Second World War and became a much loved and well-respected monarch.

* Grand Duchess of Hesse.

500-plus emperors, 2,000-plus years

From the Qin dynasty (family) in 221 BC to the end of the Qing dynasty in 1912, there were over 550 emperors (including those who ruled parts but not all) of China. Most – but not all of these – were Han people, the biggest ethnic type of Chinese person and – with China now having a population of around 1.4 *billion* people – the largest single ethnic group in the whole wide world.

Before the rule of the Qin dynasty, China had been a series of warring states. They were finally brought together under the rule of Qin She Huang,* who declared himself first emperor. He unified everything from laws and currency to weights and measures. The Great Wall of China was begun under his rule.

His dynasty was short-lived, taken over by the Han dynasty in 206 BC, and it is from this second dynasty that the Han people take their name. When the Han dynasty fell in AD 200, there followed several centuries of warfare between rival Chinese kingdoms.

* In China, the family name goes first.

The final dynasty, that of the Qing (with a 'g'), ruled from 1644 until the birth of the communist Republic of China. The last emperor was Aisin-Gioro Puyi (1906–67), who abdicated in 1912, marking the end of over 2,000 years of imperial rule.*

For a brief period, Yuan Shikai, the first president of the newly formed Republic of China, included 'Emperor of China' as one of his titles, but it didn't really stick, so doesn't count!

* Puyi wrote an autobiography which became the basis for a film made in 1987, entitled *The Last Emperor*.

Ivo of all trades

Tradition has it that the very first Norman to strike a blow against Harold's Saxon forces at the Battle of Hastings in 1066 was one Ivo Taillefer. Taillefer was minstrel knight to William the Conqueror (1027–87) who, according to legend, sang to the troops and did some pretty incredible sword-juggling in front of the gobsmacked enemy. When an English soldier ran out to challenge him, Taillefer succeeded in killing him, then – with sword flailing – he charged among the Saxons . . .

. . . only to be hacked to death.

Smokin'

Sir Walter Raleigh (c.1552–1618), who is credited with introducing tobacco to England, once claimed that he could weigh smoke. His queen, Elizabeth I (1533–1603), bet him twenty angels* that it wasn't possible.

There are three different versions of what he did next: one involves a clay pipe, another two cigars, and the version I've chosen to tell which uses just a single cigar, but the method of calculation remains the same.

Firstly, Sir Walter produced an unsmoked cigar, put it into a balance on a set of weighing scales and carefully noted its weight. Next, he lit up the cigar and smoked it, being careful to tap all of the ash from the end into the balance pan, as he went. When he'd finished, he put the small unsmoked butt into the pan, along with the ash, and weighed what was there.

The final part was easy: he simply subtracted that weight from the original weight of the unsmoked cigar, and the difference was the weight of the smoke!

* Gold coins.

Once done, it seemed so simple, but to have originally come up with such an ingenious method was quite another thing. Queen Elizabeth was extremely impressed and paid up in full.

She is quoted as having said that she knew of many alchemists 'who have turned their gold into smoke, but Sir Walter is the first who has turned smoke into gold!'

Something fishy

Queen Anne's husband was Prince George of Denmark (1653–1708). According to some, he was equally dull whether drunk or sober. He wasn't very good at conversation, which was a pity because despite being married to the queen he couldn't be king, so didn't really have much of a job. He responded to most news with the phrase, '*Est-il possible?*' This was French for 'Is that possible?', French being the language of diplomacy. Actually, he said it *so* often that this became his nickname behind his back.

Prince George suffered from asthma, causing him to wheeze loudly. One cruel courtier suggested that this heavy breathing was to let people know that he was still alive, so that he didn't get buried by mistake. He enjoyed making model boats. Charles II summed him up by describing him as 'an odd fish.'

What have we hair?

Emperor Caligula (AD 12–41) was famous for giving his horse one of the top jobs in ancient Roman government. Less talked about is that not only did he like to dress as the goddess Venus, but he also had Alexander the Great's armour stolen from his tomb, so that he could march around in the dead man's clothes pretending to be him. Despite dressing as the goddess of love, Caligula was (a) very hairy, and (b) very self-conscious of the fact . . . so much so that if anyone mentioned another particularly hairy animal – the goat – within earshot, he had them put to death.

Caligula once turned up in Rome with treasure chests crammed full of what he described as 'Neptune's treasure' (Neptune being god of the sea). When the chests were opened, onlookers were amazed to find them filled with nothing more than seashells. Everyone had to pretend to be thrilled, though, because if they *didn't* seem dead impressed they'd probably have ended up plain dead, at Caligula's hand. Caligula's name was really Gaius Caesar Augustus Germanicus. 'Caligula' was a nickname. It means 'Little Boots', after the rather nifty sandals he liked to wear.

Out of a molehill

William and Mary ruled England together from 1689 to 1694, then Mary died and William carried on ruling on his own until *he* died in 1702. Mary – as the daughter of James II – was the rightful ruler (at least, as far as the Protestants were concerned) but, as her husband and cousin, William decided that he was jolly well going to rule too. They married when he was nearly twenty-seven and she was fifteen.

Mary cried throughout the wedding ceremony, not through joy but for the same reason she burst into tears when she was told she'd have to marry the pint-sized William. Over time, though, it seems that she really came to love him. She died of smallpox, aged just thirty-two. He was killed as a result of his horse stumbling over a molehill. (He broke his collarbone and caught pneumonia.) Protestant-hating Jacobites – who thought neither Mary nor William had a right to the throne – sometimes gave a toast to the mole, referring to him as 'the little gentleman in black velvet'.

Hot stuff

Emma of Normandy (c.985–1052) was the *wife* of two kings of England and the *mother* of two kings of England. The king-husbands were Ethelred the Unready and his enemy Canute; the king-sons were Hardecanute and Edward the Confessor. Canute is famous for proving that he couldn't use his kingly power to hold back the waves and Edward the Confessor is famous for being the last king before Harold and William the Conqueror (among other things).

Late in life, Emma was accused of getting all lovey-dovey with the Bishop of Winchester so she was put on trial by her son Edward. This was no ordinary trial (by today's standards). She was required to walk in bare feet across nine red-hot ploughshares – the metal blade parts that till the soil – laid out on the floor of Winchester Cathedral.

If she survived the experience with her feet unharmed, she'd be proven innocent. If her skin burned, she'd be guilty, with more horrors to follow. She walked across the (apparently) red-hot metal without so much as a blister. In the eyes of the law, she was innocent.

As thanks, she donated nine manor houses to the cathedral's monks (one for each ploughshare). The bishop did too. You don't think . . . ? No! Surely not?

True love to the end

Edith of the Swan Neck was the girlfriend of Prince Harold who later became King Harold II in 1066. (They may actually have been married, but there's no record of it.) By the time he became king, they had four boys and two girls. Harold and Edith acted like man and wife until Harold went and married a woman called Aldgyth, who then officially became his queen. This wasn't because Harold and Aldgyth loved each other. They didn't. Aldgyth was the sister of his rivals, and he wanted to keep them happy. Not that this

mattered much. Just a few months later, Harold went and got himself killed by William the Conqueror's army at the Battle of Hastings.

It was Edith of the Swan Neck who followed her beloved Harold to Hastings to support him. (Aldgyth, meanwhile, had fled to the safety of Chester.) Edith, and Harold's mother, Gytha, watched the battle from beneath a huge oak tree, later renamed Watch Oak. When the battle was over, with Harold dead and his army defeated, it was Edith who identified his body from a tattoo. As for her name, it's probably a case of the Old English *swann hnesce* – meaning 'gentle swan' – changing over time and being corrupted to *swann hnecca* meaning 'swan neck'. No one's really suggesting that she had a particularly long white neck!

What a Silly Billy!

William IV (1765–1837) was nicknamed 'Silly Billy'. He was only on the throne for the last seven years of his life and had never expected to become king. He spent most of his life at sea as a sailor, or living with his girlfriend, Dorothy Jordan. (They had ten children together.) William went to sea aged thirteen and visited New York when America was still a British colony, making him the only British monarch ever to have actually visited North America before it became the United States. He was even a good friend of Admiral Lord Nelson.

Then, with various deaths in the royal family, he suddenly found himself wearing the crown aged sixty-four! He didn't like pomp and ceremony and wanted a really low-key coronation. It was while he was on the throne that parliament passed the Reform Act of 1832. This gave the monarchy much less power and parliament and the people much more. For the first time, middle-class men could vote. (Not just upper-class men.) William was far from happy and even dissolved parliament but, in the end, had to go with the flow. It was as a result of the Reform Act that royalty today consider themselves as being 'above politics' rather than being in the thick of it.

Silly Billy was popular with the people because he was seen as a bumbling, harmless old buffoon. He described his brother's fine collection of art as 'knicknackery', and once got upset with the King of Belgium for drinking water. 'Why don't you drink wine?' he demanded. 'I never let anybody drink water at my table!'

While other European monarchs were either being exiled or executed – think of the guillotine in France – William had bumbled happily along. For him to have a royal heir, he needed to marry someone of royal blood and to have a child. (His ten children by his girlfriend didn't count.) He eventually married but had no surviving children. When he died, his brother's daughter Alexandrina came to the throne . . . She's remembered as Queen Victoria, one of the best-known British monarchs of all history.

Tough times

Edward VI (1537–53) didn't have the easiest start to life:

- His mother, Jane Seymour (the third wife of Henry VIII), died when he was just two weeks old.

- His first stepmother, Anne of Cleves, was divorced by his father, Henry, before he'd reached his third birthday.

- His second stepmother, Catherine Howard, was beheaded – on the orders of his father – when he was four.

- His fat 'n' famous father went and died before he'd reached the age of ten.

As a nine-year-old king, Edward needed a 'Lord Protector' to help him make the big decisions and to rule in his name. This job went to his uncle, the Duke of Somerset, until – three years later – there was a power struggle and the Duke of Northumberland became Lord Protector. (Somerset, meanwhile, had his head chopped off.)

As a Protestant, Edward made changes to the Church which meant that there were suddenly far fewer priests and there was much less money to teach local children. As a result, Edward actively encouraged the setting up of grammar schools throughout the land (which is why there are still *so* many schools in England called 'King Edward VI' – and you thought it was because head teachers lack imagination).

Edward had a slow and painful death from tuberculosis aged just fifteen. The Lord Protector hushed up the boy king's death for a few days so that he could arrange things *his* way for the successor, Queen Mary.

That's *my* chair, sir!

Although Charlemagne (King of the Franks, Emperor of the Romans and ruler of much of Europe) died in AD 814, he stayed on the throne for another 400 or so years. Being dead, he didn't do much ruling in that time. His mummified body simply sat there. Then, in 1215, they finally got round to burying him . . . only to dig him up again some years later, give his nails a quick trim and give him a gold nose. Yes, a gold nose. Please don't ask me why.

Crowning glory

You don't have to be crowned straight away to be king or queen, but the crowning ceremony – or coronation – is an important part of the pomp and ceremony of kingship (as well as a chance to show off). Unfortunately for King George III (1738–1820), during his grand coronation in Westminster Abbey, the largest jewel in his crown fell out of its setting and rolled noisily across the stone floor. He did get it back, though.

Tsar Peter III of Russia had no such worries when he was crowned in 1797. He'd been dead for thirty-five years!

Your Madge!

Henry VIII (1491–1547) was the first British monarch to be called 'Your Majesty'. Only the ruling king and his queen have that title. (Nowadays, if there is a queen on the throne, her husband is not king.) Other members of the close royal family are either referred to as 'His Royal Highness' or 'Her Royal Highness' depending upon – you guessed it – whether they are a he-royal or a she-royal. Both can be shortened to 'HRH' when written down.

The famous author Henry Rider Haggard had his initials (H.R.H.) on much of his luggage which, he claimed, was often stolen because people thought they were getting a royal souvenir!

Making a meal of it

Queen Isabella of Castile and León* (1451–1504) is remembered for funding the expedition which led to Christopher Columbus 'discovering' America. He actually landed on Haiti rather than mainland North America, of course, and only discovered it for the West. (The people living there already knew about it!) The expedition may have been expensive for the day, but it can't have made a huge dent in Isabella's royal coffers. Why not? Because a quick peek at her royal accounts shows that a couple of her royal dinner parties cost about the same amount!

* In Spain.

The royal trunk

As well as many famous prisoners, including royalty, who have lived – and sometimes died – in the Tower of London, this historic British landmark has also been home to a variety of creatures including three leopards (a wedding present), some bears,* a lion and an African elephant. King Henry III (1207–72) had the biggest menagerie** in Europe at the time, set up in the Tower in 1235. The lion and the elephant had been gifts from King Louis IX of France (who had apparently acquired the elephant during the Crusades).

The elephant (the first in Britain) arrived at Whitsand in November 1254 and it was the Sheriff of Kent's job 'with John Gouch, to provide for bringing the King's elephant from Whitsand to Dover, and if possible to London by water'.

* A Norwegian polar bear was allowed to catch fish in the Thames, but with a rope around it, to stop it escaping.
** Zoo.

In preparation for its arrival, the king ordered the Sheriff of London 'that ye cause without delay, to be built at our Tower of London one house of forty feet long and twenty feet deep, for our elephant.'

Sadly, only three years after moving into the Tower, the animal died, probably as a result of the cold, the lack of space and having been given far too much red wine to drink.

Royal last orders

'The Crown' is one of the most popular names for pubs in the UK. Not far behind is 'The Royal Oak'. 'The Crown' could refer to a whole host of kings, queens, princes or princesses, which is why no pubs were given that name during the time of the Commonwealth (when Cromwell and parliament ruled, after Charles I's head was chopped off). 'The Royal Oak' refers to an oak tree that King Charles II (1630–85) is supposed to have hidden in to avoid Cromwell's soldiers before he fled to France. Many oak trees claim to be the original oak, though it's not even definite that Charles did actually hide up one. It makes an excellent story, though. And a good pub name.

Watch out!

Muggings in London are not a new thing.
Once, when walking in Kensington Gardens,
King George II (1683–1760) was mugged. The
robber took almost everything of value from
his royal personage, including George's very
fine fob-watch. *Almost* everything because
the King asked to keep the royal seal hanging
from the watch. The mugger agreed, on the
condition that the king promised not to tell
anyone. Apparently, George II kept his word
and told no one . . . so I wonder how we know
about it today?

Not much reign

One of the shortest reigns in the last 2,000 years must be that of King John I of France (15–20 November 1316). He was also known as King John the Posthumous because he was born after his father, Louis X, had already died. John's reign was short-lived because so was he. He was born king and died just five days later.

Many rumours about John's death flourished over the years. One says that his aunt killed him with a hatpin. Another says that his uncle – who became King Philip V after him – had ordered his death. Another claim was that Philip had kidnapped the real John and swapped him for a dead body.

In the 1350s, someone started claiming to be King John. He turned out to be a man named Giannino di Guccio Baglioni and he was thrown in gaol in 1360, where he died.

What the blazes?

Queen Victoria's eldest son, the Prince
of Wales (1841–1910), later King Edward
VII, loved being taken out by London's
Metropolitan Fire Brigade to see some of the
bigger blazes. The prince even had his own
fireman's uniform kept at one of the fire
stations, and he and Captain Sir Eyre Massey
Shaw* got on like a house on fire!

* Head of the Metropolitan Fire Brigade.

What a picture!

The first funeral of a British monarch to be filmed was Queen Victoria's in 1901. It was filmed by a number of different private firms including Pathé News. Most of the footage still exists today. It is all in black and white, of course, and is 'silent': filmed without sound. One of the companies, Hepworth & Co., filmed the procession at various vantage points to build up an overall picture of the day. This stretched the company's limited resources to the full, but it was worth it. Their film sold the world over, making the company enough money to become an important player in the new 'movie' business for decades to come.

You make me *mad*

When King Philip the Handsome of Spain (1478–1506) died aged just twenty-eight, his wife, Joan the Mad* (also known as Queen Joan or Queen Juana of Castile) was so upset that it was very difficult for her courtiers to pull her off her husband's dead body, which she kept on hugging and stroking.

When alive, King Philip had been wildly unfaithful to his wife and she had been wildly jealous. Now he was dead, she wouldn't let any other women anywhere near his coffin.

The funeral procession was a long one and, according to some versions of events, Joan the Mad had them stop and open the coffin a number of times along the way, so that she could once again gaze lovingly at her (dead) husband and king.

* Juana la Loca. It has since been suggested that she wasn't actually mad, simply badly treated by powerful men and possibly depressed or schizophrenic.

The bling ring

The idea of a man giving a woman a diamond ring as an engagement present, as a sign of betrothal, was started by Archduke Maximilian of the Holy Roman Empire (1459–1519) when he presented one to his wife-to-be, Mary of Burgundy, in 1477. They married later that year. Tragically, Mary died in a riding accident in 1482. The archduke became Maximilian I, King of the Romans, in 1486.

You call that *big*?

People often imagine that Britain ruled over the greatest number of countries during the time of the British Empire when Queen Victoria (1819–1901) was on the throne,* especially after she became Empress of India in 1876. In truth, George VI (1895–1952) ruled over even *more* countries than she did.

* At that time, those countries which were part of the British Empire were coloured pink on British globes and maps. The choice of girlie pink had nothing to do with there being a woman on the throne. Red was the colour associated with the Empire, but it was difficult to read the lettering of the countries' names, towns, etc. through such a dark colour, so pink ink was used instead.

Where'd he go?

Richard I (1157–99) was King of England for almost ten years but during that time only lived in the country for six months. His main home was in Aquitaine in the south of France because, as well as being King of England, he was also Duke of Aquitaine.* Also known as Richard the Lionheart or Coeur de Lion, he is remembered for going off to fight the Crusades, leaving his 'evil brother John' on the English throne in his absence. In English folklore, Robin Hood was a supporter of Richard and stood up for the poor against bad King John until the Lionheart's return.

Quite apart from the fact that Robin Hood probably never existed anyway, the truth is very different. England wasn't the country Richard loved and it wasn't simply fighting 'a just and holy war' which kept him from its shores. (His wife Berengaria – Queen of England – never so much as set foot on English soil.) England's wealth was simply a useful source of money to fund Richard's army abroad . . . which was far less romantic!

* And Duke of Normandy, and Duke of Gascony, and Count of Anjou, and Count of Maine, and Count of Nantes, as well as Lord of Ireland and Lord of Cyprus, plus sometime Overlord of Brittany.

Pearly Queen

The christening of the future King of France, Louis XIII, when he was still a prince, was a glamorous affair. His father, King Henri IV, looked splendid but his mother stole the show. Marie de' Medici (1575–1642) wore a magnificent dress covered with 32,000 pearls. And no, she didn't sew each one on herself. She had people to do that kind of thing for her.

Marie's wedding dress had been a far less impressive affair, but her husband hadn't minded . . . because he hadn't been at their wedding. He was far too busy that day! This had been a 'marriage by proxy' with Henry's uncle standing in for him at the ceremony.*

Marie de' Medici was considered a great beauty of the day, and she didn't argue with that. In fact, she commissioned the world-famous artist (Peter Paul) Rubens to paint twenty-one pictures of her, the modest lady! Rubens managed to complete them all in just two years.

When her husband, Henri, was assassinated in 1610, Marie ruled on their son's behalf – as 'regent' – until he was old enough to take control himself.

* Marrying someone who wasn't actually there wasn't that uncommon in royal circles at the time.

Maid in Britain

At her wedding to Prince Albert in 1840, Queen Victoria (1819–1901) wore large diamond earrings and a diamond necklace and had diamonds in her veil. Her wedding dress was made of satin and lace – lace which took 200 people nine months to create. Then again, it was four yards long and three-quarters of a yard wide. The veil was also made of lace, measuring four and a half yards square, and took six weeks to make. Once completed, the patterns for the lace were destroyed to ensure that the pieces really were unique. The queen had insisted that *all* the clothes she wore on this special day were made in Britain, in order to give work to her subjects.

After the wedding ceremony itself was the wedding breakfast at which the wedding cake was presented. It was 9 ft round and weighed 300 lbs, with a little model of the bride and groom on the top (which started a trend). A 167-year-old piece of the cake was put on display at Windsor Castle in

2007 as part of the celebrations for Queen Elizabeth II's Diamond Wedding Jubilee.*

The first multi-tiered wedding cake – the style with which we're so familiar today – appeared at the wedding of one of Queen Victoria's daughters.

* Sixty years of marriage to Prince Philip, the Duke of Edinburgh.

The tooth of the matter

The very first time that Queen Elizabeth II (1926–) went to hospital* as a patient wasn't until 17 July 1982, aged fifty-six. And that was to have a tooth out. She gave birth to all four of her children** at home, and was usually given medical treatment in the privacy of her palace. The hospital visit made the newspapers around the world. The New York Times announced: 'QUEEN ELIZABETH, IN HOSPITAL, HAS WISDOM TOOTH EXTRACTED'.

* The King Edward VII Hospital for Officers.
** Prince Charles, Princess Anne, Prince Andrew and Prince Edward.

In 2008, the Royal Mail broke with the convention that had existed since the world's first postage stamp, the Penny Black. Up until then, the only living people to appear on British postage stamps were royals. In this year, however, a set of stamps was produced which included the film star Christopher Lee on three of them, in three different Hammer Horror roles. In one, he appeared as the vampire Dracula, with his pointy fangs. Each of the stamps was personally approved by Queen Elizabeth. Scary teeth by royal approval . . .

On the move

Today, the body of Mary, Queen of Scots (1542–87), lies in the vaults of Westminster Abbey near those of her arch-rival Queen Elizabeth I (who signed her death warrant), but she was originally buried in Peterborough Cathedral. It was twenty-five years after her death that her son, James I, decided to have her body moved. (He'd been on the throne nine years by then, so he could have done it much sooner.)

James never really knew his mother, but ordered that 'his dearest mother [be] lifted in as decent and respectful manner as is fitting' and be taken to Westminster Abbey to offer her the same honour 'that had been done to the late Queen Elizabeth'.

In life, Mary had been a very tall woman, even by today's standards. She was six feet from head to toe. This meant that her lead coffin was very big and VERY heavy. It was carried to the abbey on a carriage pulled by six black horses.

Famously, Mary, Queen of Scots, had been a Roman Catholic, and her tomb was visited by Catholic pilgrims, some of whom claimed that, as a result of such pilgrimages, miracles took place.

Name blame

On 16 July 1917, Britain's king was a member of the House of Saxe-Coburg-Gotha. Just one day later, a member of the House of Windsor was on the throne. There hadn't been a change of monarchy, just a change of name. Britain was at war with Germany at the time yet the name of her king – George Saxe-Coburg-Gotha – couldn't look and sound much more German if it tried. This caused rumblings among the population which soon turned to real anger in some places. People were beginning to question where the monarch and his family's true loyalties lay: with their British subjects or their relatives over in Berlin?

The author H. G. Wells* wrote to *The Times* newspaper, with many a bad thing to say about George V and 'his alien and uninspiring court'. The king read the words and was enraged, saying: 'I may be uninspiring but I'm damned if I'm an alien!'

---

* Probably now most famous for having written *The War of the Worlds*, *The Invisible man* and *The Time Machine*.

Wells then wrote *another* letter in which he argued that it was time for King George to choose between his people or his 'cousins' in a public display and, if he chose his people – the British – there'd be 'a tremendous outbreak of royalist enthusiasm in the [British] Empire'.

This had the desired effect. Behind the scenes, officials frantically tried to come up with a suitable new name for the royal family. Those considered included:

 Lancaster

 Plantagenet

 Tudor-Stuart

 York

all of which had strong links with royalty of the past. In the end, it was Lord Stamfordham* who came up with the suggestion 'Windsor'. This was a new name for a British royal family but somehow sounded traditional. After all, there was already a Windsor Castle, and many people now assume that the castle got its name from the royal family, rather than the other way round!

---

* The king's private secretary.

A marriage of sorts

As the Prince of Wales, the future King George IV (1762–1830) led an extraordinary life. As a young man, he even married a commoner without the permission or blessing of his father, the king, which was therefore (in the eyes of the law) illegal. What made matters even worse was that his 'wife', Mrs Mary Fitzherbert* (1756–1837), had been married twice before *and* she was a Roman Catholic. They even lived together when huge debts forced Prinny (as he was known) to leave his own home.

Prinny would have been quite happy if she had just been his mistress (girlfriend) but Mary was having none of that. Prinny, however, was obviously crazy about her and – when he heard that she was leaving the country – pretended to have stabbed himself so that she'd come to his bedside. She did, and they ended up 'marrying'.

Prinny is famous for having the extraordinary Brighton Pavilion built in the seaside town of Brighton, now probably the city's most famous landmark, and for his drinking, eating, gambling and love of women.

* Born Mary Anne Smythe.

In 1795 he underwent an official marriage to Princess Caroline of Brunswick. This was a carefully arranged match, and the two didn't like each other very much, if at all. It wasn't long before she was living with her boyfriend in Europe, while Prinny had a string of girlfriends back in Britain.

When Prinny's father, George III, became seriously ill, Prinny ruled as regent on his behalf. Then, in 1820, the king died and Prinny became George IV. By this time he was *hugely* overweight and probably addicted to the drug laudanum.

Prinny didn't invite Caroline to his coronation which, by tradition, should have been hers too. She should have been crowned queen after he was crowned king! Instead, he gave orders that she be barred from Westminster Abbey, which she was. She came back to England

135

especially but found all the doors locked, except for one. Here, the doorkeeper said that he couldn't let her – the Queen of England – inside without an official invitation!

Just three weeks later, Caroline died of 'an obstruction of the bowel'. She left instructions that an inscription on her coffin read: 'CAROLINE OF BRUNSWICK, THE INJURED QUEEN OF ENGLAND'. The injury she was referring to wasn't the bunged-up bowel but her ill-treatment from her husband.

Riots broke out between pro-Caroline and anti-Caroline protesters in the streets of London, and again in Colchester, as the coffin began its journey back to the Continent. In the end, her supporters managed to have the inscription on her coffin as she wanted.

When George IV himself died in 1830, he was found to be wearing a locket* containing a secret picture of Mary Fitzherbert. There had been many women in his life, but she was probably the one he loved the most.**

* The king was buried wearing the locket, but the Duke of Wellington saw it, and the miniature portrait, on the body.
** Mary Fitzherbert lived until 1837. Even when no longer together, Prinny had arranged that she be given £6,000 a year for the rest of her life.

Laws on a plate

During the reign of Edward III (1312–77) a number of strange laws were introduced including one which made it illegal to have more than two courses during a meal. (Except on very special holidays, when you were allowed three.) Usually, you could have one enormous course. You could have *two* enormous courses, but it would have been against the law to have *three* courses, however small they might be!

There were also some weird laws about what clothes people could and couldn't wear. (These were added to by Edward IV and Henry VIII.) Most of these laws were repealed – dropped or altered – within a few hundred years, *except* for the number-of-courses one which was still the law of the land until Queen Victoria's reign.*

* Though people had long since ignored it and eaten what they liked when they liked.

The last shall be first

Timur the Lame (1336–1405) was born in the town of Kesh, fifty miles from Samarkand (in what is now Uzbekistan). His father was chief of a tribe of Tartars called the Berias, but they were ruled over by an overlord named Tughlak. When Timur grew up, he wanted to lead his own people without having to pay homage to some 'chief of chiefs' above him . . . so he led an uprising against Tughlak and successfully forced him out.

It wasn't long before Timur himself became the most powerful chieftain around, in effect taking over Tughlak's position as overlord, so now he set his sights even higher. In 1369, he became sole ruler of Turkestan, with his power base in Samarkand. From there, he swept his armies past the Caspian Sea, over the Ural mountains and along the Volga river, and besieged Baghdad. Once the city had been taken, 20,000 people were massacred, even those who shared his Muslim faith. Timur then went on to defeat the Egyptians and the Turks and even invaded India.* The Timurid Empire,

* From here, he sent back ninety elephants carrying loads of rare marble, from which he had a mosque built in Samarkand.

as it became known, was growing and growing.

In 1405, aged sixty-eight, Timur decided to undertake his greatest invasion yet: to conquer China. Had he succeeded, the world would be a very different place today. While preparations were under way, however, Timur the Lame caught a fever and died. Without his leadership, the Tartar soldiers simply returned to their towns and villages. The dream was over.

So where does Timur's lameness – his walking with a bad limp – fit into the scheme of things? According to legend, when the Tartars were in Samarkand arguing about who should rule, it was agreed that the first man to reach a wooden post hammered into the ground would be enthroned. No one thought Timur had a chance, but he pulled off his cap and threw it. In a graceful arc, it sailed over the heads of those running ahead of him and landed on the post before anyone else reached it. A wise old man observing proceedings said to the others, 'Your feet might have arrived before Timur's but his head reached the goal first.'

True story or not, it's a good reminder that it takes more to be a leader than being the fastest or strongest.

An embarrassment

Gladiators often fought animals in the Colosseum in ancient Rome, though not always from the safety of a gallery as the gladiator Paulus did, throwing spear after spear into the hundreds of lions released into the arena below. But it wasn't this that shocked the crowd. It was the not-so-secret secret that Paulus was, in truth, none other than the Emperor Commodus (AD 169–92), himself . . . and it wasn't becoming for emperors to play at being gladiators rather than simply watching the so-called sport.

Things got worse. Commodus started dressing like the mythological Hercules, with a lion's skin hanging down his back and its head balanced on top of his, and brandishing a big club. He became crueller and crueller and madder and madder until, finally, he was assassinated. His assassins tried poisoning him but, when that seemed not to be working, a wrestler was sent to strangle him with his bare hands.

I expect the lions would have been pleased.

The people's princess

Elizabeth, Princess of Hungary (1207–31), was a remarkable woman. Daughter of King Andrew II of Hungary, she married a German prince who became Ludwig IV of Thuringia. From a very early age, Elizabeth was aware of the suffering of people less fortunate than herself, and committed herself to helping the poor.

As well as poverty and hunger, leprosy was also spreading across Europe, brought back by Christian soldiers returning from fighting the Crusades in the Holy Land.

At first, Ludwig strongly disapproved of Elizabeth spending so much time and energy outside the castle helping the sick and hungry but then – according to legend – two extraordinary things happened.

Once, when Elizabeth was trying to smuggle bread out of the castle, he ordered her to unwrap it, knowing full well what she was up to and trying to catch his disobedient wife out! When she did open the parcel, though, instead of it being bread he was confronted with a bunch of red roses. Not only could they not have made that shape beneath the wrapping, but it wasn't even the time of year for such flowers to bloom!

On another occasion, Elizabeth had found a leper dying in the street and had helped him back to the castle, putting him in the finest bed: her husband's. When Ludwig came home and pulled back the sheet, though, he wasn't confronted by the face of the leper but – the story has it – that of Jesus.

True or not, there's no denying that Elizabeth was a selfless, caring person. When Ludwig went away on the Crusades, and the people became hungry back home, she arranged for food to be given out in the towns and cities. When supplies ran out, she used money from the royal treasury – usually spent on pomp and finery – to buy them more food. When the money ran out, she sold all her royal treasures, including the jewels from her own crown.

Many thought her mad. Others were grateful beyond words.

Sadly, Ludwig died in the Crusades and his brother, Henry Raspe, now ruled. He threw Elizabeth on to the street and, in a nasty twist of fate, forbade anyone to help her. It would be lovely to say that all the poor people who'd been helped by Elizabeth – many owed their

lives to her for saving them for starvation –
ignored the order and rallied round to help
her, but that didn't happen. Not even the nuns
dared take her in. But a handful of faithful
servants didn't desert her, finding scraps to
live off where they could. In the end, her
uncle, Egbert, a bishop, set her up in a new
home.

When many of Ludwig's friends returned from
the Crusades, they were horrified by the way
that Elizabeth had been treated by her dead
husband's brother, and insisted she be allowed
to live back in the castle. She did for a while,
but soon decided to become a nun.

She spent the last few years of her life, once
again, helping the sick and the elderly.
Amazingly, she was only twenty-four when
she died in 1231. A year later, the Pope
declared her Saint Elizabeth of Hungary.

Frederick the Great's not-so-great dad

Frederick William I of Prussia (1688–1740) is probably best remembered for being the father of Frederick the Great, but he treated his son appallingly. Frederick William often beat the boy for no real reason. Young Frederick took up playing the flute to try to lose himself in the music, but this was taken away from him when his father discovered that he was planning to run away not only from home but also from Prussia, heading for either England or France! That wasn't the only punishment, though. As well as being deprived of his flute, Frederick William also had Frederick locked up in Kustrin Castle . . .

. . . and, as if *that* wasn't bad enough, the king even thought about having his son executed. This was the fate that befell the young officer who'd helped Frederick to plan his escape, and Frederick was forced to watch him die.

Frederick William I had the reputation of being 'a parade ground general'. In other words, he built up an impressive-looking army – spending three-quarters of Prussia's revenue on it – but never really took it into battle.* He did, however, get a reputation for kicking women in the street.

In the end, Frederick William released his son from the castle in return for him marrying a foreign princess and, before he died, the father–son relationship did improve . . .

. . . but it could hardly have got much worse, now, could it?

* He increased the size of the Prussian army from 38,000 to 89,000 men, often having men kidnapped and forced to train as soldiers!

145

Too much of a good thing

When Emperor Joseph II of Austria (1741–90) first heard Mozart's opera *The Marriage of Figaro* he commented, 'Too many notes, Mozart!' Nowadays, this comment is often used as a jokey example of the Emperor not recognizing the work of a musical genius but, in fact, Joseph was really reflecting the musical taste of the time. Many people, including 'experts' (and even his friends), thought that the young composer crammed so much into his scores that they sometimes suffered from musical overload!

Some achieve greatness

Catherine the Great of Russia (1729–96) wasn't born Catherine and she wasn't born Russian, either. Her name was Princess Sophia Frederika Augusta of Anhalt-Zerbst but as a small child she was usually called Figgy!

Figgy and her mother visited Moscow at the invitation of the Empress Elizabeth (famous for having 10,000 dresses and 10,000 shoes).* Figgy's mum was excited at the prospect of visiting Russia because she knew very well that when Empress Elizabeth died, the Empress's nephew, Peter, would become the Tsar of Russia . . . and he was currently fifteen years old, the same age as Figgy. Could the Empress possibly be thinking of a royal marriage?

Figgy and her mother certainly arrived in Moscow in style in a convoy of thirty sleighs, each pulled by sixteen horses.**

* That was 5,000 left shoes and 5,000 right shoes, making 5,000 pairs in total.
** Making a total of 480 horses, each jingling with sleigh bells!

147

It was the Empress Elizabeth, a formidable old lady, used to having her own way – and her word being law – who changed Sophie's name at their first meeting. 'I shall rename you Princess Catherine,' she said. So the girl was neither Figgy nor Princess Sophia Frederika Augusta of Anhalt-Zerbst any more!

When the now-called-Catherine first met Peter, she was surprised how young he looked, but they soon became friends.* Tragically, the boy caught smallpox and, although he was lucky enough not to be killed by the terrible disease, his face was left in a dreadful pock-marked, pitted, state and all his hair fell out. Despite this, Catherine married him and did her best to help him train to be a good Tsar one day.

Sadly, Peter's tutor had a very strange method of trying to get him to learn. When the boy got an answer wrong, he would be made to stand in a corner with a picture of a donkey hung around his neck.

* They talked to each other in French, a language they both understood.

Peter became mentally unstable and started beating servants and torturing animals. When Empress Elizabeth died in 1761, Peter became Tsar . . . and an extremely unpopular one at that. He ordered all priests to shave off their beards, and he seized money from the Church, claiming that it was rightfully his.

One day, when the Tsar was away with his German officers, the Royal Guard took Catherine to the cathedral where she was proclaimed Empress of All The Russias. On hearing the news, Peter simply quit, signing 'a letter of abdication'. Perhaps he was 'persuaded' to sign. No one knows for sure. What is known is that it was later announced that he'd been killed in an argument with the guards.

Catherine claimed that she'd had nothing to do with her husband's death, and the Russian people seemed to believe her, or were simply relieved that Tsar Peter was no more and didn't care how he had met his death. Either way, Figgy ruled Russia successfully for thirty-four years, and gained the name of Catherine the Great.

My kingdom for a horse

When Henry VIII's third wife, Jane Seymour, died (after giving birth to a son), Henry looked around for wife number four. He was looking not only for a wife who'd bring him more power and authority – the daughter of a foreign king, for example – but also for one he'd find physically attractive.

When he heard about Christina, Duchess of Milan, she sounded like a real possibility. Both Emperor Charles of Spain and the French King Francis were interested in Milan, so if he married Christina, that would give him real bargaining power. He sent the artist Hans Holbein to paint her, to get an idea of what she looked like. Henry liked the look of her (or at least the portrait of her), but the marriage didn't take place.

Next, Henry had Holbein paint Louise and Renée, the two sisters of the Queen of Scotland, but nothing came of them either. Finally, in desperation, Henry's adviser, Thomas Cromwell, told him about Anne of Cleves (c.1515–57), a beautiful woman from a wealthy and important family in Flanders.

Once again, Hans Holbein was despatched with his paint and brushes and, once again, a painting made its way to the royal court for Henry's approval. He agreed with Cromwell's appraisal, finding her portrait most attractive, and arrangements were made and terms agreed for the marriage.

When Anne arrived in England, there was no going back. Henry wasn't in a position to offend all the powerful people and families involved in this royal marriage . . . the only problem was that he discovered that the real Anne of Cleves looked nothing like the woman in the portrait! He went so far as to describe her as looking like a horse: he referred to her as 'the Flanders mare'!

So, although the marriage went ahead as planned, it was very short-lived. Fortunately for Anne though, her head remained firmly attached to her body. In fact, she did extremely well out of the marriage. In the divorce settlement, she received:

 a manor house

 a castle

 a palace

their entire contents

 a generous yearly allowance

 and the specially made-up (and rather meaningless, yet strangely endearing) title of 'the King's Beloved Sister'.

When Anne's family asked her to come home, she chose to stay in England and managed to remain on good terms with Henry for the rest of his life, seeing him marry twice more.

She outlived the king and was buried in Westminster Abbey.

Some bad 'uns, by George!

King George I (1660–1727) was the first of the Hanoverian kings of England, who came over from Germany to rule. He didn't even bother to learn English and was generally unpopular with the British people.

His son, the Prince of Wales – later George II (1683–1760) – made an effort to speak the language and was far more popular than the king.

George I got fed up with living in England so he went back to Germany for a while in 1716, leaving his son in charge as 'Guardian of the Realm'. If countries could sigh with relief, this one did, and the younger George became more and more popular.

On one occasion, the Prince of Wales directed operations to put out two fires which had broken out in London, showing real leadership and bravery. When it was all over, he sent £1,000 – a very large sum of money back then – to help the victims.

On another occasion, when a lunatic tried to assassinate him at the Drury Lane Theatre, the audience was mightily impressed at how calm he remained as the would-be assassin was dragged away.

It was while George I was away that young George and his wife Caroline had their first son, Frederick. When George I returned to England, one of the first things he did was to make the Duke of Newcastle the boy's godson. The Prince of Wales *hated* the Duke, and his father knew it. He'd appointed him Frederick's godson out of spite.

When the younger George argued with his father over the matter (in English, which his father didn't understand), the King had the prince and his wife thrown out of the palace, forcing them to leave their children behind.

This made the Prince of Wales a bitter, angry man. By the time he became King George II in 1727, he was nothing like the popular young Prince of Wales he had once been, though he did take ruling the country as a serious responsibility.

As for Prince Frederick, under his grandfather's guidance he'd become an unpleasant gambling drunkard. Now a feud grew between him and *his* father.

King George II described his eldest son as 'a monster' and 'the greatest villain that ever was born'. Queen Caroline, his mother, described him as 'the greatest ass and the greatest liar and the greatest beast in the whole world', and even wished him dead, though she – a teeny-weeny bit more diplomatically – actually said: 'I most heartily wish he was out of it.'

Britain was then plunged into war with Spain and France, and George II also had to deal with Bonnie Prince Charlie, the Young Pretender, who claimed that he had more right to be on the English throne than some German.

George II lived until the ripe old age of seventy-six in 1760, making him older than any other British king who'd ruled before him.

But what about Frederick, Prince of Wales? Did he become king on his father's death? No, because nine years previously, he was hit on the head by a cricket ball and, not long after – whether the accident had anything to do with it or not – he died. His father had outlived him, something which would no doubt have pleased his mother, Queen Caroline, no end had she herself not died way back in 1737.

Hats off to George and Charlie!

George III (1738–1820) and his wife, Charlotte, were crowned King and Queen of England in Westminster Abbey in 1761. They were so popular that extra seating had to be brought in for the ceremony, including wooden boxes built on top of tall scaffolding, high up against the stone columns. (Because these boxes offered such a good view, people were charged fifty guineas – a huge sum of money – to hire one.)

After the coronation, the couple took Holy Communion. Normally, people would take their hat off for this, so the congregation was waiting to see if the newly crowned king would take off his crown . . .

. . . which, much to their delight, he did. This made him *even more* popular, because it showed that he was 'humble before God'.

Things didn't go so smoothly for Queen Charlotte, though. She tried to follow her husband's lead and take her crown off too, but it got all tangled up in her hair so she couldn't.

Rock bottom

After George III and Queen Charlotte's coronation in 1761, they held a special banquet which is remembered for all the wrong reasons. Firstly, it's rumoured that one of the guests was Bonnie Prince Charlie. If the Stuart family had still ruled England – as they did up until the death of Queen Anne in 1714 – then Bonnie Prince Charlie would have rightfully been king.

But because those in power get to write history, Charles Edward Stuart (as he was also known) *wasn't* seen as the rightful heir to the throne but as another 'pretender.* Which is why Bonnie Prince Charlie was also known as the Young Pretender . . .

Whether he was actually at the coronation banquet or not will never be known, but the rumour that he'd somehow managed to sneak in was embarrassing enough.

* Pretending that he had the right to wear the crown.

157

The other memorable event at the banquet (which happened for sure) involved the Lord Steward's horse. When the Lord Steward appeared on horseback before Their Majesties, the horse was trained to walk backwards when he was leaving their royal presence. (The idea was that it would be rude to turn your back on the king, which was why, in many situations, people would walk out of rooms backwards, while bowing.) At the banquets, however, the horse decided to *back up* to King George and Queen Charlotte *bottom first*. What a bummer!

Are we nearly there yet?

When Richard II (1367–1400) was crowned king in 1377, he didn't go back to his palace after the coronation in a carriage or on horseback. He was carried by a certain Simon Burley. It wasn't that Burley was particularly burly,* it's just that Richard was only ten years old and he was very, very tired. Richard II became King of England when his grandfather, Edward III, died. His father** was already dead.

The day before his actual coronation, young Richard had to ride from the Tower of London to Westminster (where he'd be crowned in the abbey the following day). It was a very slow procession and involved girls of about his age sprinkling gold leaf on his hair and throwing pretend gold coins in front of his horse as he rode by.

Richard was dressed in white and had been put on a white horse. Everything was designed to show up his youth and purity (while,

---

* Burly = beefy, muscular, well-built.
** Known as the Black Prince because of the black armour he wore.

behind the scenes, his uncles planned to wield the real power and to rule the country in the way *they* wanted).

At the coronation itself, there was much rubbing of his body with ceremonial oils and, to top it all, he was loaded up with the trappings of the royal insignia. These included (in alphabetical order):

 alb

 armilla

 buskins

 crown

 imperial mantle

 ring

 rod

 sceptre

 spurs

 sword

 tunicle.

No wonder the lad was exhausted and worn down by it all. As for that Simon Burley who carried him home at the end, he was the king's tutor.

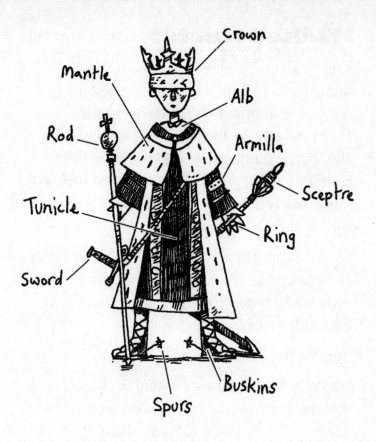

Crown

Mantle

Alb

Rod

Armilla

Tunicle

Sceptre

Sword

Ring

Spurs

Buskins

Wicked uncle?

There's a very famous story about the hunchback Richard, Duke of Gloucester (1452–85), murdering 'the Princes in the Tower' so that he himself could become king. The 'Tower' in question was the Tower of London but only one of the so-called princes was actually a prince. The elder of the two was, in fact, already king.

As for his hunchback, Richard probably didn't even have one, so – like much in history – what really happened will probably never be known for sure.*

Here's what we *do* know:

Twelve-year-old Edward V and his younger brother were staying in the tower at the request of their uncle Richard, Duke of Gloucester. Prince Edward had been in Ludlow in 1483 when his father, King Edward IV, died and he became Edward V. It was necessary for him to come to London because this was the 'seat of power' where he would be crowned, and it made sense for good old Uncle Richard to look after him and his brother.

* For example, it is sometimes said that, unusually for a baby, Richard III was born with teeth!

Young King Edward travelled as far as Northampton in the care of his governor of the household, Lord Rivers. There, the Duke of Gloucester had Rivers arrested, and went back with the boy to London, where the younger prince soon joined him. The Duke then locked them both up and declared himself Richard III, King of England . . .

. . . and soon after that, the two boys – er – disappeared.

So things don't look great for Richard III (formerly Duke of Gloucester) in the 'but-I-was-innocent' stakes, but if there was any damning evidence to prove his guilt it's either long gone, or yet to be found.

The current Duke of Gloucester – who became duke in 1974 – is president of the Richard III Society, founded in 1924 under the name of The Fellowship of the White Boar.* Its aim is to show that Richard III wasn't quite the villain he was made out to be. There are now a number of other societies also dedicated to reassessing Richard and any 'misconceptions' there might be about him.

* That's 'boar' as in wild pig, not as in 'boring!'

One thing's for certain: Shakespeare painted Richard III in a very bad light in his play of the same name.

And the name of the young prince who, along with his king-brother, was most likely murdered in the Tower? He was called Richard too, but I saved mentioning that until the end because that makes it all the more confusing.

A couple of Cromwells

A vulture may not be seen as the noblest of creatures – it lets others do the killing, then feeds off the carcass – but a titmouse must come even lower down in the pecking order of impressive beasts. And these were the two animals to which Oliver Cromwell (1599–1658) and his son Richard were compared in the comment: 'The vulture died and out of the ashes rose a titmouse.'

After the execution of King Charles I in 1649 and a bloody civil war between the pro-Parliament Roundheads and the Royalist Cavaliers, Oliver Cromwell had become Lord Protector of England in 1653. (Charles I's son, the future King Charles II, had fled the country and was living in France.) Cromwell was offered the title of 'king' but he turned it down. He did, however, end up living in a palace (Hampton Court).

A couple of days before he died, he told his ministers that he wanted his son, Richard, to become Lord Protector after him. Just because he wasn't king and he was all for Parliament running the country, that isn't to say that he was against the idea of his son inheriting the throne – er, I mean, his job as boss of England.

The prospect of Tumbledown Dick or Idle Dick (as Richard was nicknamed) becoming the new Protector can't have filled the men's hearts with glee. He already had a reputation for not being the brightest penny in the purse, and he soon lived up – or down – to it. Parliament gave Richard Cromwell the staggeringly huge sum of £60,000 to pay for his father's funeral but he somehow still managed to spend much, much more than that and went into debt. In May 1659, he quit his job as Protector and ended up fleeing the country.

Ironically, after all the trouble and expense of burying his father, Oliver Cromwell's body was later dug up by the Royalists (once Charles II was on the throne). In 1661, the dead Cromwell was tried and found guilty of treason. His body was hung from chains in Tyburn. Later, his head was stuck on a stick outside Westminster Hall for over twenty years, and his body was thrown into a pit.

His head finally got a second burial, but not until almost three hundred years later, in 1960.

Seeing red

William the Conqueror's son, King William II of England (c.1060–1100), was better known as William Rufus – 'rufus' meaning 'red' – because of his red hair and face. Yup, he had a red face. Not like a tomato, or red with embarrassment, but as in having a 'ruddy complexion'. He's most famous for either being mistaken for a stag and shot, or for being killed by an arrow which hit a stag and then glanced off on to him and killed him, *or* for being murdered and the whole I-was-aiming-at-a-stag being a cover story (aka 'a pack of lies'). Whatever happened, it actually took place during a day of hunting in the New Forest in 1100.

The man who shot him was Sir Walter Tyrrel, who, after the event, fled the country and ended up going to the Holy Land on a pilgrimage, supposedly out of guilt for having accidentally killed his king. William Rufus's body was found by a charcoal burner who heaved it on to the back of his cart and wheeled it off to Winchester Cathedral, where the local monks were far from thrilled to receive it. The king had not only been a very cruel man but had also been very rude about Christianity, so the monks buried him as quickly and with as little fuss as possible. He certainly didn't get all the pomp and ceremony you'd expect at the funeral of a king.*

Rufus didn't have a son to inherit the throne so, when he died, his brother Robert Short-Trousers (Curthose) should rightfully have become king. (In fact, Robert was *older* than him, but that's another story.) As well as wearing short trousers at the time, though, Robert was also out of the country fighting a Crusade.** This gave the next in line (younger

* A few years later one of Winchester Cathedral's towers fell down. The monks blamed it on bad luck caused by having such an un-Christian king buried in holy ground.

** Apparently, Robert's trousers weren't short as in 'above-the-knee' but short as in 'from-waist-to-ankle' because he had short, stubby legs!

brother) Henry the chance to seize the throne . . . but he had to act quickly. Just four days after brother Rufus's unfortunate death, Henry had got his hands on the keys to the royal treasury *and* managed to get himself crowned King Henry I at Westminster Abbey.

Robert tried to claim the throne but ended up spending the last twenty-eight or so years of his incredibly long life* as Henry's prisoner. He took the time to learn Welsh.

* Robert Curthose lived to be eighty, which was a very, *very* old age at the time.

Musical chairs

In May 1659, Oliver Cromwell's son Richard (1626–1712) gave up the role of Lord Protector. He fled to France but later settled in Italy. There he lived under the assumed name of 'John Clark', without his wife (who'd stayed behind). With Idle Dick (as he was often known) gone, talk soon turned to bringing back the monarchy. Charles II, son of the beheaded King Charles I, was back on the throne by the following year.

Idle Dick did eventually return to England in the reign of William and Mary (by which time Charles II had died and his brother, James II, had been forced to give up the crown in favour of his daughter Mary, and Mary's husband, William of Orange).

Richard lived in a little house in Chelsea.

In 1709, by which time James II's second daughter Queen Anne ruled England, the story goes that Richard Cromwell went to see a royal ceremony, with Anne seated on the throne. When another onlooker commented, 'Have you ever seen such a sight before?', the very old and poorly dressed ex-Lord Protector is supposed to have replied, 'Never since I sat in that chair!'

Hats off to Henry!

Henry VI (1421–71) was crowned three times, but only twice as King of England. The second coronation was as King of France. Here's how it went:

Date:	Place:	Crowned:
6 Nov 1429	Westminster Abbey	King of England
16 Dec 1431	St Denis, Paris	King of France
25 Oct 1470	St Paul's Cathedral*	King of England again

Henry VI was the youngest ever, ever, *ever* King of England. He came to the throne in 1422 when he was just nine months old. He didn't get to be crowned, the first time round, until he was eight.

When his grandfather (on his mother's side) Charles VI of France died, the French throne passed to him, hence his being crowned King of France when he was ten.

---

* Not the domed St Paul's Cathedral (where I was christened), which wasn't officially completed until 1711, but an earlier cathedral on the same site (destroyed in the Great Fire of London in 1666).

171

Sadly, in 1453, Henry VI had a mental breakdown, so Edward, Duke of York, was made 'protector' and ruled the country on his behalf. (By this time, the French had won all but Calais back from their English rulers.)

Unfortunately for Henry, when he got better in 1455, Edward of York was in no hurry to give him his power back . . . A civil war followed between Edward's Yorkists and Henry's Lancastrians, which became known as the Wars of the Roses.

Despite Henry VI being alive and well, the victorious Edward of York managed to get himself crowned King Edward IV in 1461. Henry fled the country but, on his return, was captured and imprisoned in 1465.

In 1470, his supporters managed to free him and have him crowned a second (or third) time, but he was far from well. His fragile mental state hadn't been helped by his being locked up for years. When he was rescued from the Tower of London by the Earl of Warwick, Henry was found to be 'amazed and utterly dulled with troubles and adversities' but it was a figurehead – a rightful king – in whose name he could govern that Warwick was after. It might even have been useful that the king himself didn't really know what was going on around him.

Just six months later, Edward IV was back on the throne and Henry was murdered, aged forty-nine.

Meet 'Joe Bloggs'

The last King of France, Louis Philippe (1773–1850), and his wife Queen Marie, had to flee the country during the French Revolution to avoid having their heads chopped off.* They fled to England in disguise. He called himself 'Mr Smith' and she called herself 'Madame le Brun' . . . which is French for 'Mrs Brown'!

* During the French Revolution, heads weren't chopped off with an executioner's axe but with an especially designed machine called the guillotine, named after Dr Joseph Guillotin who designed it.

Look but don't touch

King Mongkut* of Siam** (1804–68) – made famous in the musical and film *The King and I* – had many, many titles. These included:

 Brother of the Moon

 Descendant of Buddha

 Half-Brother of the Sun

 Possessor of the Twenty-four Golden Umbrellas

 Supreme Arbiter of the Ebb and Flow of the Tide.

* Also known as Rama IV.
** Thailand.

It was decreed that he should never be looked at directly – but not paying him full attention could result in either:

(a) being put to death instantly; or:

(b) having to cut hay for the sacred (white) elephant.

No one could touch royalty, which is why everything had to be passed to the king on a golden platter. It is also why, in 1910, when a Siamese queen was drowning, her servants stood respectfully by and did nothing.

Bling! Bling!

King Louis XIV of France (1638–1715) liked to wear flashy clothes. *Really* flashy clothes. He had a robe encrusted with real diamonds. Lots of them. So many diamonds, in fact, that just six robes like it would have been enough to pay for the building of the whole of the Palace of Versailles . . . and that's one flashy palace!

A likely story!

John O'Groats is a name usually spoken in the same breath as Land's End. While Land's End is right down in the far, far south-west of England (in Cornwall), John O'Groats is in the tip of the north Scottish mainland.*

In fact, John O'Groats, the place, is named after John de Groot, who was a Dutchman! King James IV of Scotland (1473–1513) granted de Groot the right to run the ferry between mainland Scotland and the island of Orkney (which, until recently, had belonged to Norway).

John de Groot was a member of a large, wealthy family. According to legend, there were eight different people claiming that it was *their* right to be the head of the family and, therefore, *their* right to sit at the head of the table (the most important position) and *their* right to have their own private entrance, and the best room, overlooking their lands.

* To me, this is a real Scottish-sounding name, perhaps because groats (as well as being an old type of coin) contains the word 'oats', the main ingredient of one of Scotland's most popular dishes: porridge.

178

John de Groot finally solved the problem –
and showed up the ridiculousness of the
situation – by building a house with eight
equally large windows, eight equally
important entrances, and an octagonal – yup,
that means eight-sided – table where each of
them could sit with equal importance. That's
the story, at least.

The house, with its eight large windows and
eight doors, certainly seems to have existed,
but the legend may well have grown up
around its appearance. In other words, the
story was created to fit the architecture,
rather than the other way round. Either way,
de Groot's name lives on as one of Britain's
most famous landmarks and it makes a potty
enough story to be included in this book!

When all is said and done . . .

King George III (1738–1820) is famous for being mad. There's even a well-known play by Alan Bennett called *The Madness of George III*,* which later became the film *The Madness of King George*. It was while George III was on the English throne that the British North American colonies declared their independence on 4 July 1776, something which made George seriously consider giving up his crown.

In the end he didn't abdicate and, in 1785, he even officially received America's first Ambassador to England, John Adams, saying, 'I was last to consent to the separation but the separation having been made and having become inevitable, I have always said, as I say now, that I would be the first to meet the friendship of the United States as an independent power,' which doesn't sound crazy at all. It was rather statesmanlike, in fact: rather *regal*.

* There was a story going around at the time that the number 'III' was dropped from the title of the film because people would think that it meant that there were two other *Madness of King George* films before it – numbers I and II. The truth was that, in America – a huge market for the film – George III was known as plain old George.

Oh, fancy rat!

George II (1683–1760) and his wife, Queen Caroline (1683–1737), were very keen that the child of their son and heir, Frederick Prince of Wales, should be born at their palace, Hampton Court. The eager grandparents wanted to be there for the birth. It wasn't that they were particularly fond of Frederick or his wife, Princess Augusta. They weren't. They just wanted to be absolutely sure that the baby really was Augusta's. (Their nickname for the prince himself was 'Changeling' because he was so unlike the rest of the family: slim, when they were plumptious.) What a trusting family.

The Prince of Wales *hated* the idea of his first child being born in his parents' home so, when Princess Augusta went into labour, he managed to smuggle her out of the house and took her on a bumpy 12-mile coach ride to their own home in St James's, London. While the rest of the family were back at Hampton Court, playing cards in blissful ignorance, the princess gave birth to a daughter, named Augusta after her.*

* If you think Princess Augusta having a daughter called Princess Augusta is confusing, this second Princess Augusta went on to have a daughter called Caroline, who became another Queen Caroline, married to another King George . . .

Queen Caroline was furious when she heard the news and demanded to see the girl. When she laid eyes on her granddaughter, she had no doubt that she was their son's child. 'If, instead of this poor, little ugly she-mouse, there had been a brave, large fat, jolly boy,' she said, 'I should not have been cured of my suspicions.'

If you think calling little Augusta a little ugly she-mouse was rude, one of her courtiers went one better, describing her as 'a little rat of a girl' no bigger than a 'large toothpick case'!*

* I sympathize. There was only one entry in my own baby book. It read: 'bedraggled rat'.

That sinking feeling

The pride of Henry VIII's navy was the mighty *Mary Rose*. After a refit, the warship's weaponry included:

 two (standard) cannons

 two demi-cannons (medium-sized cannons)

 two culverins (even smaller cannons)

 six demi-culverins (yet smaller cannons)

 two sackers (about the size of a culverin)

 one falcon (a light cannon)

in addition to which, when it went to face a French invasion fleet in 1545, it also had 600 armed soldiers on board (as well as the 100-man crew).

The idea of cutting holes in the sides of ships to fire cannons through was a relatively new one, so the *Mary Rose*'s ability to fire broadside – sideways on – made it a powerful enemy.

King Henry VIII (1491–1547) himself watched with satisfaction as the ship set sail until it suddenly tipped to one side and sank beneath the waves of the Solent (the stretch of water between mainland Britain and the Isle of Wight). Hundreds drowned.

The wreckage of the hull of the *Mary Rose* was finally brought back to the surface some 437 years later, in 1982.

Big things come in small packages

The smallest Queen of England – as in 'least tall' – was Queen Matilda (c.1031–83), wife of William the Conqueror. She was originally said to be 4 ft 2 in tall but, in 1959, her bones were examined by experts who determined that she must have been around 5 ft tall.

Matilda and William were cousins, so the Pope had been against their marrying each other. He was much happier when they both had abbeys built as penance.

There are two different versions about the lead-up to their marriage. One has it that on hearing that Matilda refused to marry him because she was far more 'high born' than him, the Duke of Normandy (as William was in those days, before he invaded England) rode from Normandy to Bruges. He found Matilda on horseback on the way to church. He yanked her off her mount with her long braids of hair, and dragged her down the street, before riding off.

Despite this outrageous behaviour, Matilda agreed to marry him and so ended up queen, bearing him eleven children (including the future kings William II and Henry I).

Just four months before William, as Duke, invaded England, he and Matilda 'gave' their daughter Cecily* to God. In an important ceremony at the abbey of La Trinité at Caen – attended by all the local bigwigs – the young girl became a nun. They wanted God on William's side.

Matilda and William had a long and apparently loving marriage, until she turned against her husband and supported her eldest son, Robert, against him. When she died in 1083, William's personality is said to have taken a real turn for the worse. This small woman's death was a big, big loss.

* Just seven years old at the time.

A matter of life and death

When Edward VIII (1894–1972) gave up the English throne in 1936 to marry American divorcee Wallis Simpson, he was created Duke of Windsor and ended his days living in France. Although his wife became the duchess, she was not awarded the title 'Her Royal Highness' but this didn't stop his referring to her in that manner, and insisting that everyone around him did the same.

When the duke became ill and it was clear that he wouldn't live, he was visited in his final days, in May 1972, by the current monarch, Queen Elizabeth II, and the Prince of Wales.

The duke's doctor was given very specific instructions by the British Ambassador before the visit: the Duke of Windsor could die *before* the royal party arrived. He could die *after* the royal party left. But there was *no way* the duke was allowed to die *during* the royal visit.

Fortunately for the doctor, the duke died eight days after the Queen had left!

A spot of bother

When, in 1701, King James II of England (who was also James VII of Scotland) died in exile in France,* the King of France declared that James's son, James Stuart** (1688–1766), was now the rightful king of England. Declaring him to be 'James III' (which would also have made him James VIII of Scotland), King Louis XIV sent the twenty-year-old lad off to Scotland to try to claim the crown.

James had planned to land in the Firth of Forth, but anything and everything seemed to turn against him.

Firstly, the weather was terrible during his crossing of the Channel. Secondly, he was expected, so the English fleet was ready and waiting for him, led by Admiral George Byng. Thirdly, his own fleet decided to turn tail and run (or whatever it is that ships do under the circumstances). The last straw for the would-be king was that he'd caught the measles . . .

. . . so he went home!

* The Catholic king had been replaced by the protestant King William and his wife Queen Mary.
** Later known as The Old Pretender.

Favourites

Queen Victoria's favourite grandchild was Frederick William Victor Albert of Prussia (1859–1941), better known as 'Kaiser Bill', Emperor of Germany and King of Prussia. When, in January 1901, he learned that his beloved grandmother was dying at Osborne House,* he hurried to be at her side. There was no love lost between Kaiser Bill and the future king, Bertie, Prince of Wales,** who – on learning of his imminent arrival – sent him a telegram basically telling him to stay away.

Despite this hostile message, it was in Kaiser Bill's arms that the old queen died. He's also said to have taken charge after Victoria's death. He personally measured her body (for the coffin) and, later, even helped the royal physician to lift the body from the bed.

Just thirteen unlucky years later, England and Germany would be at war.

* On the Isle of Wight.
** Later Edward VII.

Not forgotten

Richard II's close friend, John Waltham, one-time Lord Treasurer, Lord Privy Seal, Archdeacon of Richmond and Bishop of Salisbury, was buried in Westminster Abbey in 1395, his grave bearing the inscription:

THEY BURIED HIM AMONG THE KINGS
BECAUSE HE HAD DONE GOOD TOWARD
GOD AND TOWARD HIS HOUSE

The same inscription appears on another stone in the abbey, laid some 526 years later: on the Tomb of the Unknown Warrior.

In a ceremony on Armistice Day (11 November) 1920, the remains of an unidentified body were interred in a service attended by King George V. The idea for the body of one unknown soldier to symbolize all those who had died in the Great War (many of whose final resting places were unknown) was that of an army chaplain, David Railton. In 1916, he'd come across a private garden in Armentières, France, where he found a rough wooden cross, on which had been handwritten: 'An unknown British soldier'. After the war was over, he proposed the idea of such a tomb to the Dean of Westminster.

To ensure that the body really was unidentified, the remains of four men were dug up from war graves in four of the most famous battlefields in France and Flanders: those of Arras, the Somme, the Aisne and Ypres. These were then taken to a chapel, each draped in a Union flag.* Brigadier-General L. J. Wyatt then entered the room and – not knowing where any had come from – chose one at random. The remains of the chosen soldier were then placed in a plain coffin. This was later sealed inside a more ornate one. This was then lowered into the floor of Westminster Abbey at the 1920 ceremony.

It was a year later that a black stone slab, bearing a long inscription, ending in the lines from Waltham's tomb, was laid on top.

Today, there is a tomb of an unknown French soldier of the Great War beneath the Arc de Triomphe in Paris, and tombs to unknown soldiers from a number of different wars in Arlington National Cemetery in Virginia, USA.

* The British flag, often referred to as 'the Union Jack'. Technically, it can only be called the Union Jack (as opposed to flag) when it's being used on a ship.

191

A right royal jumble

On 15 February 1952, one of the strangest events in the history of British royalty took place. The Queen of England, the dowager Queen* and the ex-King of England all attended the funeral of a dead King of England!

The dead king was George VI, a very popular king who had reigned during the Second World War. Known in the family as 'Bertie', he had never expected to become king. That was the role of his older brother, Edward. But Edward VIII reigned for less than a year, abdicating to marry the American divorcee Wallis Simpson, and passing the crown to Bertie. Outliving his younger brother, he was the ex-king. And the queen? George VI's daughter, Queen Elizabeth II.

George VI's wife, Queen Elizabeth (later 'Queen Elizabeth, the Queen Mother') blamed Edward for George's early death from the stress of being king. There was no love lost between the two sides of the family. Edward (who became the Duke of Windsor) claimed that he was 'shabbily treated'. The country's sympathy was clearly with Queen Elizabeth.

* The dead king's wife, (another) Queen Elizabeth, who rarely if ever used the title 'dowager'.

Seeing stars

Charles II (1630–85) wanted a royal observatory* – but on the cheap. It would be good to have one, but he didn't want to spend too much from the royal coffers on it. The site – the top of a hill in Greenwich, near London – was Sir Christopher Wren's** idea. But what to build it with? Penny-pinching Charles had a brainwave: recycling! He decided to use stone from an old castle on the site, and had bricks, lead and iron sent from a fort at Tilbury which had been partially demolished. That was the building materials sorted, but what about the builders? They'd have to be paid. There was some spoilt gunpowder in the armoury which the king had sold for an impressive £500, so he used that for wages! He still had to pay John Flamsteed an annual sum of £100 to be the first Astronomer Royal, but made him pay for his scientific instruments and staff himself.

* A building designed and equipped with telescopes to study stars, planets and space.
** Best remembered today for having designed St Paul's Cathedral in London, the one with the dome, and where I was baptized in 1962.

Making a splash!

Despite being married to Queen Catherine (1638–1705), King Charles II had many mistresses,* the most famous of whom – and his favourite – was the actress Nell Gwyn (sometimes spelled 'Gwynne'). Many of his mistresses gave birth to his children. Nell had one child by the king who survived to adulthood, described as being 'a very pretty boy'.

At first Charles refused to name him, and there are stories that, after six or so years, Nell had finally had enough and threatened to throw the boy into a lake/moat/river** if he didn't get not only a name but also a title. (Not throw *herself*, note, but their child!) Whatever really happened, something did the trick because the boy henceforth became Charles Beauclerk, Earl of Burford (1670–1726). Eight years later, in 1684 when he was fourteen, the king also made him the Duke of St Albans.***

* Girlfriends.
** Depending on the version you choose to believe.
*** This was the last dukedom Charles created in his reign.

His Majesty also gave Charles two impressive-sounding roles (which didn't really require any effort on his part): Master Falconer of England and Registrar of the Court of Chancery, with a very acceptable salary of £1,500 per year.

Nell Gwyn, on the other hand, got neither a noble title nor an official income (though the king did pay her £100 a year). She was, however, at one stage, a Lady of his wife's Privy Chamber! There is some suggestion that he'd planned to make her the Countess of Greenwich but he died, in 1685, before he had the chance to do so. His deathbed instruction was, 'Let not poor Nellie starve.'

Charles's brother, James II, did as the late king asked, not only paying off her huge debts but also giving her an income for life. As it turned out, 'life' was only for two more years. She died in 1687.

The Duke of St Albans, meanwhile, became a soldier, rising to the rank of colonel, and – when James II was kicked off the throne for being a Catholic and replaced by William and Mary – he became loyal to the new monarchs, gleaning a whole host of new titles and appointments, including:

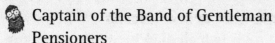 Captain of the Band of Gentleman Pensioners

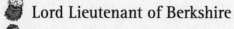 Lord Lieutenant of Berkshire

Fellow of the Royal Society

Knight of the Garter.

Charles married Lady Diana de Vere and they had nine sons and three daughters. Six of their sons became Members of Parliament for Oxford.

Number one son

When King Charles II died, his brother James became king. It's not that King Charles didn't have any children. He had plenty. The only problem was that none of them was the child of his wife Queen Catherine. They were all born 'out of wedlock', meaning that they were the children of his mistresses (girlfriends). His favourite mistress was the actress Nell Gwyn, but his favourite son was the Duke of Monmouth (1649–85), whose mother was someone called Lucy Walter.* By all accounts, Monmouth was stunningly handsome.

When King Charles died in 1685, Monmouth decided to claim the English throne. Because his uncle, now James II, was a Catholic, and a far less popular person than he was, he really thought that he was in with a chance of seizing the crown and keeping it.

* Some claim that Charles and Lucy actually married, which would have put the cat among the pigeons!

He landed in Lyme Regis in Dorset, on England's south-west coast, and went inland to a place called Taunton, where he had himself declared king. In next to no time, 4,000 people turned up to support him, and they marched on the city of Bristol which they spectacularly failed to take, so he faced King James's army at Sedgemoor and was badly defeated there instead. He fled to the New Forest where he was soon found and dragged off to the Tower of London.

Monmouth wasn't a prisoner for long. That same year he was beheaded.*

* It took five blows of the executioner's axe.

Don't say you weren't warned

George I (1660–1727) was a very superstitious man and was once told by a fortune-teller that he would die within a year of burying his wife. When his wife, Sophia, eventually died in 1726, he decided that he might be able to cheat death by not having her buried! He stalled for six months but finally decided that he must go to Hanover to make arrangements for her funeral.

Filled with dread, he said goodbye to his family, fearing that he'd never see them again . . .

. . . and how right he was. On his way, he had a stroke in his coach and was taken to his home in Osnabrück, where he died in the very room where he had been born.

199

A spectacular send-off

Protestants William and Mary ruled jointly as king and queen when her father, James II, was booted off the throne for being a Catholic. When Mary (1662–94) died, William (1650–1702) ruled on alone as William III. Mary's funeral was an extraordinarily grand affair.

Beforehand, her embalmed body lay in state in Whitehall, illuminated by 30,000 – yes, 30,000 – candles.* She died of smallpox in December 1694 during a bitterly cold winter when the Thames froze over, and wasn't buried until March the following year, which allowed plenty of time for making the lavish arrangements.

Two hundred poor elderly women were supplied with black gowns so that they could become mourners in the royal funeral procession. In addition, thousands of yards of black cloth were distributed among people well in advance, in the hope that they too would wear black and attend the proceedings.

* 300 glass chandeliers with 100 candles each.

The funeral itself took place at Westminster Abbey and, for the first time, was attended by members of both the House of Lords and the House of Commons.

When William died seven years later, his funeral was a far cheaper, less well-attended affair.

'A surfeit of lampreys'

Henry I (1068–1135) went against doctors' advice and it killed him. He was warned against eating lampreys* and then promptly proceeded to eat a vast dish of the things. Lampreys were considered a real delicacy (in much the same way caviar is today); so much so that every Christmas the king was traditionally presented with a lamprey pie by the loyal subjects of Gloucester. And, boy, did Henry love those slimy things!**

The trouble with lampreys, however, is that they have to be carefully prepared before cooking: they have poisonous filaments which must be cut off. It's possible that this particular dish wasn't prepared properly for him.

It was a slow death. It took Henry a week to die, giving him plenty of time to put his affairs in order, including plans for his own funeral.*** Henry died in Normandy and, in order to preserve his body on the journey back to England, it was sewn inside a cowhide.

* Eel-like creatures.
** The lampreys, not the people of Gloucester.
*** He was buried in Reading Abbey, where he'd originally laid the foundation stone for its building.

His eldest son William having died in a shipwreck, Henry stipulated that his daughter Matilda should rule. Things weren't so simple. What in fact followed was 'the Anarchy': a time of civil war.

Give me a ring

King Edward the Confessor (c.1004–66) is famous for wearing a sapphire ring which became his symbol. In many pictures of the king, his particularly large ring is clearly shown. According to legend, when he was walking past Westminster Abbey one day, the Confessor gave it to a beggar.

Years passed and some English pilgrims in the Holy Land were approached by the 'beggar' who revealed that he was, in reality, St John (who wrote the gospel),* and that he wished them to return the ring to Edward. He also wished them to deliver a message to the king: a warning that he would die within six months (which, apparently, Edward did).

The ring was duly returned to Edward and he wore it until his death and beyond. He was buried with it on his finger. When Edward himself was declared a saint, his body became even more important. (Miracles were often said to occur at the tombs of saints.)

His coffin was opened thirty-six years after

* If he really was St John, this would have been a miracle. John had lived at the time of Jesus, over a thousand years previously.

his death, in 1102. Apparently, his body was so perfectly preserved that it looked as if he'd only been recently buried. The Bishop of Rochester gave the Confessor's snowy white beard a good tug, in the hope of gathering a few saintly beard hairs, but not only did he fail to get a single one, he also got told off by the abbot of Westminster Abbey where the body had been buried!

In 1163, the coffin was opened again when it was moved to a new shrine especially built for the Confessor's tomb. This time the all-important sapphire ring was removed from his finger and put in the abbey treasury for safe keeping . . . and no one seems to be sure exactly what happened to it next.

Some claim that the sapphire on top of the Imperial State Crown – still worn by the British monarch on special occasions – is the original sapphire, and it's often referred to as the St Edward Sapphire. If this is true, then that would be an amazing link between distant and modern royalty.

As for Edward the Confessor's ring-free remains, they were moved around a few *more* times and in 1685* some scaffolding collapsed and landed on the tomb, splitting it open. Before anyone could stop him, a choirboy reached inside, unceremoniously rummaged around among the bones and pulled out the Confessor's crucifix which was presented to King James, who was delighted!**

* At the coronation of James II.
** Sadly, when Catholic James II fled the country in 1688, he only went and lost it!

Spot the difference

After King Charles I was beheaded, Oliver Cromwell (1599–1658) became Lord Protector and, famously, turned down the offer of becoming king. In many eyes, this made him a man of the people. That's as may be, but what's often forgotten is that he lived in a palace (Hampton Court), was addressed as Highness,* wore purple clothes** edged with ermine, and – oh yes – travelled in the royal coach and sat on a throne. But he wasn't actually *king*, you understand.

P.S. His son inherited the job when he died.

* A king is addressed as 'Your Majesty', a prince as 'Your (Royal) Highness.
** Purple being the colour of emperors and kings.

Filling in the blanks

When the future James II was still Duke of York (the younger brother of King Charles II) his first wife, Anne, died, and he decided to remarry. In the end, he was left with the choice of two women (neither of whom he'd actually met): thirty-year-old Leonora, and Leonora's fifteen-year-old niece Mary of Modena* (1658–1718). Both actually wanted to become nuns, but that didn't bother James. What James wanted, James got.

He sent his representative, Lord Peterborough, to Modena (in what is now Italy) with an important mission: to decide which woman he thought James would prefer and then to marry them by proxy. In other words, there would be a marriage ceremony with Peterborough standing in for James.** To speed things up, Peterborough took a marriage licence with him with a blank space on it where he could simply add the name of the woman he chose for James. He chose Mary, the wedding-by-proxy took place, and the pair returned to England for Mary to meet her husband.

* Many people got married long before they were fifteen back then.
** Royal marriages by proxy weren't that unusual.

It was tough for Mary. James was twenty-five years older than her and had two daughters from his previous marriage. She was also unpopular with the people of Protestant England: she, like James, was a Catholic.

When Charles II died in 1685 and James became king, Mary became pregnant and there was a fear that they'd have a son who would be another Catholic king one day. Sure enough, they did have a son. Rumours soon spread that Mary had never been pregnant at all – that she'd been faking it – and that someone else's baby had been smuggled into the palace in a bed-warmer*. That way, they could be sure of a Catholic 'son and heir'.

Things soon turned from bad to worse. In a matter of years, James II found himself losing the throne to his own daughter (also called Mary) and her husband, William.** Mary of Modena, meanwhile, fled to France with their child James Stuart, who later returned to England to – understandably! – attempt to claim the throne as rightfully his. He became known as the Old Pretender.

* A metal covered pan – on the end of a long wooden handle – which could be filled with hot coals.
** Who governed jointly as William and Mary.

King of kings

When Mary Tudor (aka Bloody Mary) became Queen of England (she was Mary I, and shouldn't be confused with Mary, Queen of Scots, or Mary II who ruled later with her husband William as the royal combo William and Mary) she married Prince Philip of Spain (1527–98). This made Philip 'king consort'. In other words, he was king because he was married to a queen. By the end of his life, he was also the king of:

 Angola

 the Azores

 the Canaries

 the Cape Verde Islands

 Central America

 Ceylon (Sri Lanka)

 Florida

 Goa

 Guinea

 Macao

Milan

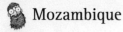 Mozambique

 Naples

the Netherlands

Portugal

Sardinia

Sicily

South America

Spain

the West Indies

and the Philippines, which were named after him.

To put it another way, he ended up ruling one of the world's largest empires, with territories on every single continent known to Europeans at the time.

Tom Tom

In the days of King Henry VIII (1491–1547), the name 'Thomas' was either:

 very common

 one which Henry *really* liked (or which saved him having to bother to remember other names)

 a name given to particularly intelligent and ambitious people; or

 none of the above*

because the king seemed to surround himself with Thomases. There were:

 Cardinal Thomas Wolsey (Lord Chancellor)

 Thomas More (Lord Chancellor)

 Thomas Cromwell (chief minister)

 Thomas Cranmer (adviser and Archbishop of Canterbury)

which must have been very confusing sometimes, to say the least.

* And the whole thing was one of those amazing coincidences.

The unexpected crown

King John (1167–1216) probably never
expected to be king. He was the youngest
of eight children. Three of his elder siblings
were female so 'didn't count' when it came to
inheritance – boys came before girls – but that
still left four elder brothers who were in line
for the throne ahead of him. Not only that, if
one of them had a son (which one did), they
might be entitled to the crown, not him.

Not only did no one ever believe John would
be king one day, his father Henry II didn't
even bother to give him any real money
or land. His brothers got land, but not
him . . . hence his nickname (among others),
Lackland.*

But by the time his brother Richard the
Lionheart had died, all of his other brothers
were dead too, and John claimed the throne.
He was readily accepted by England and
Normandy, but there were others who believed
that his nephew, Arthur – the son of one of

* The nickname may also have had something to do
with the fact that he lost a lot of English territory to
France during his reign, and, in effect, gave England
over to the power of the Church.

213

John's elder brothers* – should rule.

Things went from bad to worse and at one stage Arthur attempted to kidnap John's mother (his grandmother Eleanor of Aquitaine) but ended up being captured by John's forces instead.

What happened next was strongly disputed at the time. Some claim that Arthur died at the shock of the 'orrible things that were about to be done to him; others that John got drunk, killed Arthur, weighed the body down with stones and threw it either into the moat of the castle he'd been imprisoned in or into the River Seine. Whatever the truth, it was convenient for John that this fellow claimant to the throne of England was now out of the picture.

All that was left was Arthur's sister, Eleanor, the 'Fair Maid of Brittany'. Just to be on the safe side, he had her locked up for the rest of her life.

* This was John's brother Geoffrey, who died before he himself had a chance to rule.

A faithful following

Edward VII's funeral was held on 20 May 1910 and attended by the crowned heads of Europe – including the German Emperor and no fewer than eight kings – as well as royalty and dignitaries from across the globe including the President of the United States.

Surprisingly, however, the first to follow the gun carriage – on which his flag-draped coffin rested on its journey to Paddington Station where it would be loaded on to the royal train to Windsor – was Caesar.

No, not Julius Caesar. That would be silly. Impossible.

No, *this* Caesar was the late king's dog, a fox terrier, who was probably wondering where his master had gone.

London calling

Britain's first royal Christmas broadcast – which today is the Queen's Christmas Message – was heard on Christmas Day in 1932. The medium was radio and the speaker was King George V (1865–1936).

The idea came from Sir John Reith, known as the 'founding father' of the BBC,* as a particularly ingenious way of promoting what was to become the BBC World Service,** a radio network intended to spread 'British values' across the globe.

The royal broadcast was introduced by a sixty-five-year-old shepherd named Walton Handy from Ilmington Manor in Warwickshire, with carols from the local church choir and even bell-ringing.

The broadcast reached an estimated 20 million people and was declared a great success.

* Which was the British Broadcasting Company before becoming the British Broadcasting Corporation.
** Originally the Empire Service.

A conscience of sorts

William III (1650–1702) had been brought over to England from Orange (in the Netherlands) along with his wife Mary II to rule England as a Protestant monarch in place of the Catholic King James, which made him far from popular with the Catholics (who made up most of Europe).

In 1696 – two years after Mary's death – a group of Catholic conspirators, led by Sir George Barclay, planned to kill William at a river-crossing at Turnham Green during a hunt. This would be a brief window of opportunity when the king would be separated from his guards.

The conspirators might have got away with it if someone on the fringes of the plot hadn't got in touch with the king urging him not to go hunting – it was against his religion to let a murder happen without at least a warning!

As a result, the king's life was saved but the conspirators were less fortunate. Most of the ringleaders were put to death, though Barclay went into hiding and died peacefully in France in 1710.

Make cathedrals, not war!

Kings often spent money – and squeezed their subjects for more – in order to fight wars. It was almost expected of them. King Henry III (1207–72), however, was more interested in spending money on buildings . . . in a *big* way.

His pet project was improving Westminster Abbey. This was for the glory of one of his predecessors, Edward the Confessor, and, like Edward the Confessor, Henry was a peace-loving king. Henry also encouraged or inspired the building or renovation of cathedrals at Winchester, Salisbury, Peterborough, Wells and Lincoln.

He also gave plenty of money to his various relatives, many of whom came over from France.

In the end, the barons had had enough. They agreed to release more funds to the king but only if he would be more accountable, with the creation of a form of parliament: in other words, if they themselves were given more power and recognition. Henry III had to agree. This agreement became known as the Provisions of Oxford.

Henry's problems with the barons weren't over, though. He ended up fighting the barons, led by Simon de Montfort, and was captured by them at the Battle of Lewes in 1264. For a time, it was the barons who ruled England, and not the monarchy. Henry's son, Prince Edward, had been captured too but later managed to escape. At the Battle of Evesham in 1265, Prince Edward defeated de Montfort and his father, Henry, was freed.

When Henry III died in 1272, his body was, very fittingly, temporarily placed in the tomb of Edward the Confessor at Westminster Abbey while his own tomb was prepared.

A triple tragedy

When, as a prince, Edward I (1239–1307) was away from England on the Crusades, accompanied by his wife Eleanor of Castile, three messengers arrived from home with three reports of death.

The first informed him of the death of his elder son, Henry.

The second informed him of the death of his second son, John.

The third informed him of the death of his father, King Henry III, meaning that he was now King Edward I of England.

It is said that Edward took the first two pieces of news very calmly but was obviously deeply upset with the third, sobbing unashamedly. When asked why this was, he is said to have replied, 'A man may have more sons, but never another father.'

Brotherly love. Not

King Canute had a son named Harold Harefoot
with his first wife Queen Elfgifu and one
named Hardecanute* with his second wife
Queen Emma (who'd been married to the late
great King Ethelred the Unready). Though
half-brothers, Harold and Hardecanute didn't
exactly get on. Harold ruled as King Harold I
and, on his death, was succeeded to the throne
by Hardecanute.

One of the first things Hardecanute did was
to dig up his dead brother's body, cut off his
head and lob it into a bog!**

* Aka Harthacnut, among many other different
 spellings.
** It was later salvaged by a fisherman.

Over my dead body

Before Henry I died, the English throne
had been promised to his daughter Matilda
(1102–67) but it ended up being claimed
by his nephew Stephen.* During Henry's
lifetime, Stephen had sworn allegiance to
him and agreed that Matilda should be queen
on Henry's death. Henry granted Stephen
huge amounts of land and property in both
England and Normandy, making the young
man fabulously wealthy . . .

. . . but this didn't stop Stephen wanting *more*
and going against his word. No sooner was
Henry dead than he claimed the crown for
himself. Many Norman barons who'd also
sworn allegiance to Matilda declared support
for Stephen. One of the reasons for this was
that this was an age when people felt that it
was a man's right to rule and that the country
would be all the stronger for it.

* Henry was a son of William the Conqueror, and
Stephen was the son of William's daughter, Adela.

In fact, years of in-fighting followed with battles lost and won. During this time of turmoil and civil war, Matilda made two dramatic escapes. Firstly, she escaped from Devizes in Wiltshire, in 1141, disguised as a dead body. Dressed in a funeral shroud, she was laid on a bier – a stand for corpses – and tied to it. Then she was simply carried by her supporters past the enemy without suspicion.

On the second occasion, a year later in a bitterly cold December, she escaped from St George's Tower in Oxford Castle (which was being besieged by Stephen's forces). She lowered a rope from her window and successfully made the perilous descent. Then, dressed in white to blend in with her snowy surroundings, she and a group of knights skittered across the icy surface of a frozen river and then made a thirteen-mile journey to safety.

In the end, she gave up and left England forever. Her son did, however, succeed to the throne of England on Stephen's death, and ruled as Henry II.

Nice one, Henry!

One of England's best-remembered victories against the French was the Battle of Agincourt, in which an English force of 8,000 defeated French forces of 50,000 in 1415. The hero of the hour was the English troop's leader, King Henry V (1387–1422).

News of the victory reached England before he did, so when Henry stepped off his ship at Dover he was greeted by wildly enthusiastic crowds. They were *so* enthusiastic, in fact, that the front of the throng swarmed into the sea and he was carried, shoulder high, on to the beach. But the welcome didn't end there. Thousands upon thousands of people came out to line the route of Henry's march to London.

When the king arrived at Blackheath, on the outskirts of the capital, he found that, along with the ever-swelling crowds, the Lord Mayor, nobles, archbishops and clergymen had all assembled to greet him there, rather than wait for him to reach the city.

In London itself, the public celebrations were like nothing ever seen before. Even the fountains flowed with wine.

Little man!

Queen Elizabeth I (1533–1603) died from infected tonsils. It was a slow business, with her taking weeks to die. She drifted in and out of consciousness, with her courtiers desperate for her to name her successor (for, having never married and had children, there was no water-tight copper-bottom shoo-in to the throne). She spent much of the time out of bed but, when her Secretary of State, Robert Cecil, insisted that 'to content the people' she must go to bed, Elizabeth snapped, 'Little man! Little man! The word *must* is not to be used to princes!'

As for her successor? It was James, the son of her arch-rival Mary, Queen of Scots, whose death warrant she had signed.

Name game

Queen Elizabeth II and her husband, Prince Philip, Duke of Edinburgh (1921–) are:

 third cousins

second cousins once removed

fourth cousins once removed.

Both have Queen Victoria as their great-great-grandmother.

Prince Philip's full surname was Schleswig-Holstein-Sonderburg-Glücksburg and, when Elizabeth married him, some or all of it might have become her name too!

It was the Home Secretary – who went by a rather unusual name himself, that of Chuter-Ede – who came up with the solution. He suggested that Prince Philip take the name of his English uncle, Lord Mountbatten,* so he did just that, becoming Philip Mountbatten in 1947. As it turned out, the Queen chose *not* to adopt his name on marriage later that year, and stuck with Windsor. In practice, out of

* Mountbatten is, itself, a changed name. When the British royal family decided to change their name to Windsor, they also changed Battenburg to Mountbatten.

respect, most of their descendants now refer to themselves as 'Mountbatten-Windsor' (when not using their titles such as Wales* or York**).

Prince Philip is the oldest and longest serving of all consorts (husbands or wives) of a reigning British monarch.

* Charles, Prince of Wales.
** Prince Andrew, Duke of York.

What's in a name?

People often confuse the United Kingdom, Great Britain and the British Isles. Today, the United Kingdom is England, Scotland, Wales and Northern Ireland. Great Britain is England, Scotland and Wales. The British Isles are England, Scotland, Wales, Northern Ireland *and* the Republic of Ireland too.

It was King James I of England who came up with the term Great Britain in 1604. He was already James VI of Scotland when he became the English king and – being king of both (along with Wales) – decided to combine the roles into one. In a pastiche of the wedding vows, he said, 'What God has conjoined, let no man separate.' But he didn't end the analogy there. He went on to say, 'I am the husband and my whole isle is my lawful wife.'

The union was not official until the Act of Union in 1707, during the reign of Queen Anne, with the formation of the United Kingdom (at this stage excluding Northern Ireland). The union with Ireland came in 1801 . . . but the troubles between Britain and Ireland were far from over.

The Queen's 'old granny'

Mary of Teck (1867–1953) was born during Queen Victoria's reign in the same room of Kensington Palace where Victoria had been born. A great-granddaughter of George III, Mary was due to marry the Duke of Clarence in 1892 but, just six weeks before the wedding, he died of pneumonia, so it was agreed that she marry Clarence's brother, the future George V, instead.

Their wedding took place in 1893, when Victoria was still on the throne. Though obviously a marriage of convenience, it seemed a happy one. On the death of Victoria, George's father, Edward VII, ascended to the throne. In 1910, she became Queen Mary when George became king. She outlived him to see her eldest son become Edward VIII in 1936, but not to see him crowned. He abdicated before any coronation could take place, and the crown passed to Mary's second son, Bertie, who reigned as George VI. Meanwhile, her younger son, the Duke of Kent, was tragically killed in a plane crash. Having lived through the First World War and Edward's exile, she now lived through the Second World War, only to see Bertie die of cancer in 1952. She died in 1953 with her granddaughter, Queen Elizabeth II, on the throne and only weeks away from her coronation.

She had lived through the reign of six monarchs.

Taking charge

When William II (aka William Rufus) was accidentally (-on-purpose?) mistaken for a stag and shot dead, the rightful heir to the throne of England was Robert, Duke of Normandy. But he was busy fighting a Crusade, so his youngest brother, Henry (1068–1135), decided that he'd rather like to wear the crown . . . but he had to act *fast*.

Within moments of Rufus's death, Henry was galloping to the royal palace at Winchester where, with a bit of sword-waving and rabble-rousing – he was a popular guy – he managed to get his hands on the keys to the royal treasury. That done, he headed for London and, within three days of William II's death, declared himself King Henry I.

He knew that his brother Robert would want the crown for himself, so Henry needed to make himself as kingly as possible and as popular as possible before his arrival.

In just three months, he'd:

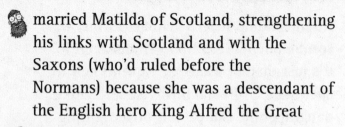 married Matilda of Scotland, strengthening his links with Scotland and with the Saxons (who'd ruled before the Normans) because she was a descendant of the English hero King Alfred the Great

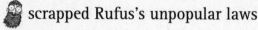 scrapped Rufus's unpopular laws

brought the popular Archbishop of Canterbury, who'd been treated so shabbily by Rufus, back from France

expelled the more corrupt and unpleasant nobles (pulling down their illegally constructed castles)

established himself as being firm but fair.

When Robert did finally show up with his army, Henry used his skills and diplomacy to defuse the situation. Instead of fighting, they hugged and made up!

Over time, though, Robert started causing trouble so, in 1106, Henry decided to put a stop to it. He invaded Normandy, defeated his brother* and ended up being the Duke of Normandy too.

---

* Henry kept Robert prisoner for the rest of his life, and he lived until he was a staggering eighty years old!

'I've got the king!'

No one can accuse William the Conqueror's son Stephen (c.1092–1154) of not being brave. It's just that he was a pretty useless king and spent much of his reign fighting Matilda, daughter and named heir of the previous king, Henry I. Stephen ruled for longer than Matilda, but she did have her moments.

One such occasion was in 1141 in a mini-battle just outside Lincoln (which was really more of a military skirmish). In the middle of the fight, when things seemed to be going well for Stephen's men, he decided to get down off his horse and join the melee. He was hacking away with his huge sword with such vigour that it broke, so he snatched up a battleaxe and started whirling it about, slaughtering anyone in its path . . . until this broke too.

One of Matilda's knights, William of Cahagnes, took the opportunity to pounce on Stephen and grab him by the helmet, shouting, 'Come here, everybody! I've got the king!' In next to no time, King Stephen was clapped in irons/put in chains and taken away.

First, he was taken to Gloucester so that Matilda could laugh and point at him and rub his nose in his defeat. Next he was taken to a dungeon in Bristol.

But Stephen had the last laugh. Within nine months he was released, and he reigned for a further thirteen years.

Don't call me 'Al'!

A question I often ask classes of schoolchildren is 'What was Queen Victoria's first name?' The answers I usually get include:

(a) Elizabeth

(b) Queen*

and (after a teacher has whispered in someone's ear):

(c) Victoria.

In fact, Queen Victoria's first name was Alexandrina (and, as a princess, she was known as 'Drina'). She was named after one of her godfathers, Alexander I, Tsar of Russia.

The very first time Victoria was announced as Queen – after the death of her uncle, William IV – it was as 'Queen Alexandrina'. But never again. After that, it was as Queen Victoria, and anything from her age is referred to as Victorian, not Alexandrinian!

* This is the most common reply in the USA!

Falling apart

Henry V (1387–1422) died on the outskirts of Paris but had expressed instructions that he be buried in Westminster Abbey. In those days, the journey would have taken a few weeks, so a way had to be found to preserve his remains. He could, of course, have been embalmed but the decision here was to cut his body into manageable-size chunks – I hope you haven't just had lunch? – and to boil his flesh off his bones. The cleaned bones were ceremonially placed in a lead coffin and taken back to England.*

It wasn't just Henry's body that suffered dismemberment. According to Westminster Abbey's own website, the silver head and hands of the effigy of Henry that lay on top of his tomb were stolen in 1546. The head and hands on view today were added in 1971 and are made of polyester resin.

* As to what happened to the fleshy water (a kind of royal cannibal soup), I've no idea.

Royal flush

George II was the last British monarch to be buried at Westminster Abbey. Since then, with two exceptions,* Britain's kings and queens have been buried in St George's Chapel, Windsor.

George's wife, Queen Caroline, died twenty-three years before him but, on his death, one side of her coffin was opened and one side of his coffin was removed. This way they could, in effect, share one big coffin inside a stone sarcophagus.

Slightly less romantic was the fact that George had died of a heart attack in Kensington Palace . . . while sitting on the loo.

* Queen Victoria is buried in the Royal Mausoleum, Frogmore, near Windsor; Edward VIII is also buried in Frogmore, but in the Royal Burial Ground.

237

Cheers!

Queen Victoria's son, Edward VII (1841–1910), had many, many, many girlfriends. As Prince of Wales, what seems to have mattered to him most was having *fun*. Even when he was married to Queen Alexandra, he spent a lot of time with other women.

When visiting the Moulin Rouge – a famous Paris nightclub with plenty of drinking and dancing girls – the well-known dancer La Goulue would welcome him with a cry of ''Ullo, Wales!'

This would be a signal for the Prince of Wales to order champagne for the orchestra and dancers. Speaking of which, Edward is also known to have bathed in champagne!

Not quite a worldwide web

The Emperor Heliogabalus (c.203–22) – real name: Varius Avitus – introduced the cult of the Syrian sun god to Rome, hence the nickname.* What's less well remembered is that he was an avid collector of cobwebs. He wasn't interested in the size or design of them, or which kind of spider had made them. He was interested in the amount – the *weight* – of his collection.

He ended up with 10,000 lbs of them. Why? Because he could. It was to show that he was so important and so powerful that he could waste people's time collecting them for him. Still, he probably ended up with the heaviest cobweb collection in the ancient world . . .

* 'Helios' comes from the Ancient Greek word for 'sun'.

I'm dropping u . . .

The French emperor Napoleon Bonaparte (1769–1821) wasn't actually French himself. His parents were Corsican and he was born in Corsica, a Mediterranean island off Italy. His name was actually 'Buonaparte' but he dropped the 'u' to make it look less Corsican and more French . . .

. . . not that this really mattered because he's one of that rare breed of people who are well-known by just the one name. These include Churchill, Gandhi and Chaplin.*

Even more unusually, he's equally well known by just his first name or his last name.

About the only other person instantly identifiable by just their first name is pop star Madonna . . . and she didn't have a set of laws named after her** or invade Moscow.

It was while Napoleon was 'Emperor of the French' that Nelson's fleet beat the French fleet at the Battle of Trafalgar in 1805, and he was 'Emperor of France' when Wellington beat him at the Battle of Waterloo in 1815.

* Pop star 'Sting' doesn't count because it's a nickname.
** The Napoleonic Code.

240

Feeling green

Emperor Napoleon (1769–1821) spent his final years in exile on the island of St Helena, under the watchful eye of his British captors. He arrived in 1815, having been exiled on the island of Elba the previous year (by the French this time) and having escaped.

The English governor of the island was Sir Hudson Lowe and he and Napoleon hated each other on sight. When Napoleon became ill in 1818, Lowe thought he was faking. When in 1819 Napoleon was in such pain that he couldn't eat, Lowe thought he was exaggerating. When Napoleon died on 5 May 1821, Lowe realized that – er – he hadn't been.

There were three theories as to what killed Napoleon Bonaparte:

1. stomach cancer (the official British explanation);

2. an ulcer (which would have been embarrassing, because ulcers could be dealt with, so he needn't have died from it);

3. wallpaper.

Yes, a very popular theory in later years was that the green wallpaper in Napoleon's rooms poisoned him. The beautiful green colour was made with arsenic (which is a poison). The theory goes that the paper got damp and gave off poisonous arsenic fumes which, slowly but surely, killed him over time.

There are those who believe in the arsenic idea but think that the death was an accident. (Arsenic was used to colour many things green in those days.) And there are those who believe that the British deliberately poisoned Napoleon that way.

If so, it's probably the first example of assassination by wallpaper!

Who was given the boot?

Napoleon Bonaparte (1769–1821), Emperor of France, may have lost the Battle of Waterloo, and the Duke of Wellington may have won it, but it's Napoleon's name which is associated with brandy* – a popular alcoholic drink – while Wellington's name is given to – er – a type of boot.

* Napoleon' is a term given to brandy aged for four or more years.

Sticks and stones

William, Duke of Normandy, William the Conqueror and King William I of England (1027–1087) were all titles for the same man: the one who became England's first Norman king after defeating King Harold at the Battle of Hastings in 1066. He used to have a far less glamorous title (more of a nickname, really). It was 'William the Bastard'. His father, Robert,* wasn't married to his mother, a tanner's daughter. A tanner is someone who gives leather that nice brown colour, and the most common way of doing that involved animal poo. This made William a bit of a joke with the local Norman nobles. Robert couldn't marry William's mother (he was *far* too important for that) but made sure that she was looked after by a chap called Viscount Herluin of Conteville. She and the viscount had a number of children, including one called Odo (making him William's half-brother). Odo later became Bishop of Bayeux, and it was he who ordered the making of the famous Bayeux Tapestry – which isn't actually a tapestry – showing all the key events in the Norman Conquest and the events leading up to it.

* Nicknamed Robert the Devil, and later the Duke of Normandy.

All four one!

As well as being called 'George' and being kings of England, Georges I, II, III and IV had something else in common.

They all died on a Sunday.

A foiled attack

In 1974, an attempt was made to kidnap
Queen Elizabeth's only daughter, Princess
Anne, from her car. Her personal bodyguard,
chauffeur and a passer-by were all shot by
the would-be kidnapper, Ian Ball. He then told
Princess Anne to get out of the car, to which
she replied, 'Not bloody likely!'

Later, the princess reported, 'I nearly lost my
temper with him, but I knew that if I did, I
should hit him and he would shoot me.'

The princess was then helped to escape by a second passer-by, who punched Ball in the back of the head and led her to safety. When Ball regained his senses, he shot his fourth victim, a passing policeman. By now, back-up had been called for and Ball was finally stopped and arrested.

All those shot survived.

In a secret document,* the then prime minister, Harold Wilson, wrote that Princess Anne showed 'quite extraordinary courage and presence of mind'.

* Released to the public in 2004 after the 'thirty-year rule'.

Working in the lab

Charles II (1630–85) was a keen amateur scientist. In his famous diary, Samuel Pepys writes about going to see 'the King's Elaboratory* underneath his closet' in 1685. He describes it as a 'pretty place' and that he saw 'a great many chemical glasses and things, but understood none of them'. (The lab wasn't under Charles's cupboard or wardrobe. By 'closet', Pepys meant the King's bedroom.)

It was in this laboratory that Charles created some of his famous medical preparations, the best known being 'King Charles's Drops'. In 1694, a Dr Lister wrote: 'The late King Charles not only communicated to me the process, but also showed it to me himself by taking me alone to his elaboratory in Whitehall while the distillation was going on.'

Exactly what these drops had in them is unclear, but the ingredients certainly seem to have included ground-up human bone.

* So now you know how the word 'laboratory' started out.

Which is witch?

Before becoming King James I of England as well, King James VI of Scotland sailed to Denmark in 1589 to marry Princess Anne, sister of the Danish king. On their return journey, they were caught in such a bad storm that their ship had to seek shelter in Norway for a number of weeks. Rumours soon started to fly that the storm had been summoned by witchcraft. Suspects were rounded up in both Scotland and Denmark.

Over a hundred people were arrested, accused of witchcraft, in North Berwick, Scotland, alone. Some confessed to having met with the Devil himself in a church and using his powers to try to poison members of the royal household and to sink the king's ship. Then again, they were horribly tortured, so may well have been willing to confess to anything.

James was fascinated by the North Berwick witch trials. He even had one supposed 'witch', Agnes Sampson, brought to Holyrood Palace where he interrogated her personally.

A contemporary source claimed: '[She] confessed before the King's Majesty sundry things which were so miraculous and strange as his Majesty said [she and the others] were all extreme liars, whereat she answered she would not wish his Majesty to suppose her words to be false, but rather to believe them . . . she declared unto him the very words which passed between the King's Majesty and his Queen at Oslo in Norway the first night of their marriage [in private] . . . whereat the King's Majesty wondered greatly, and swore by the living God, that he believed that all the devils in Hell could not have discovered the same, acknowledging her words to be most true.'

She was executed. King James now actively encouraged witch hunts and decreed in 1604 that those found guilty should be put to death.

Over the following eighty years, there were over 2,000 witch trials, resulting in deaths of thousands of so-called witches (both men and women).

Toeing the line

In many countries, kings and queens were seen as trend-setting celebrities. What they did or wore often became fashionable. King Charles VIII of France (1470–98) was one such monarch. He wore square-ended shoes, so his fashionable courtiers started wearing square-ended ones too . . . What most of them *didn't* know was that he wore them for comfort, not style: he had six toes on one foot!

Known as 'Charles the Affable',* he died as a result of hitting his head on top of a doorway during a game of real tennis!**

* Easy and pleasant.
** An indoor game which existed long before today's lawn tennis.

Don't mess with Mary

According to John Foxe in his *Book of Martyrs* (1563) – and he could have been biased, of course – rather a lot of Protestants were put to death for their faith on the orders of 'Bloody Mary' (1516–58), aka Mary I of England,* the Catholic queen. The total number was put at 314, and included:

 2 boys

 2 infants

 5 bishops

 8 gentlemen

 9 virgins

 21 divines

 25 wives

 84 artificers**

 100 husbandmen, servants and labourers.

* Aka Mary Tudor (*not* to be confused with Mary, Queen of Scots).
** Skilled workers.

Many of them were burned at the stake.
Many others who weren't actually killed were
horribly tortured.

Mary's father was Henry VIII, who broke away
from the Roman Catholic Church in the first
place.

Touched French royals

The seventh-century King Clovis II of France is said to have gone mad as a direct result of having stolen the arm of a martyr, but you wouldn't guess that from his nickname. He was known as Clovis the Lazy. (Maybe arm-theft was an easy option.) His great-grandson, Childeric III, however, was always seen as a bit of a dimwit, hence the nickname Childeric the Idiot.

Around 500 years later, King Louis IX of France's mother thought he was of unsound mind. He was known as Louis the Saint, because he was canonized.* Louis's poor youngest son – Robert of Clermont – certainly went mad, and with good reason. During a tournament, he was hit over the head with an iron weapon called a mace.**

* Officially declared a saint by the Church. As the only French king to be canonized, many places were named after St Louis . . . including – er – St Louis in the USA.
** Though some people may try to tell you that it was a sledgehammer.

In the fourteenth century, Charles VI of France actually had the unambiguous nickname of Charles the Mad. Sometimes poor Charles either didn't know who he was or who his wife and children were. Once, he killed members of his own company with his sword, believing them to be the enemy. He went through phases of believing that he was actually made of glass and, to avoid breaking – as glass is inclined to do – he had iron rods put inside his clothing to form a protective frame around himself.

Putting a (full) stop to it?

There is a story that the Empress of Russia, Maria Fedorovna (1847–1928) – wife of Tsar Alexander III – once managed to save a convicted man from almost certain death by the simple use of punctuation.

The Tsar had been asked to pardon the man, but Alexander refused this, writing: '*Pardon impossible, to be sent to Siberia*', followed by his royal signature.

The Empress managed to change the entire meaning of the letter simply by scratching out the existing comma and replacing it with a new one in a different position.

Her husband's signed note now read: '*Pardon, impossible to be sent to Siberia.*'

True or not – and the Empress was known for her charitable works – it makes a great story *and* shows the importance of punctuation!

Pride before a fall

King Louis XI of France (1423–83) was a great believer in astrology – reading the future from the stars – but even he became a little uneasy when a certain astrologer so accurately predicted the death of a servant girl. Was it safe having someone with so much knowledge at large? Might not such a man become too powerful?

Louis – or so the story goes – decided that it might be best if the astrologer be removed from the situation. He was summoned to the royal apartments and, on arrival, was snatched up by the king's servants and rushed over to an open window, from which he would be dropped from a significant height.

Before King Louis gave the final nod that he be thrown to his death, he couldn't help asking the astrologer one final question: 'Do you know when you will die?'

'Yes, sire,' the astrologer replied, his head already outside the window. 'I shall die just three days before Your Majesty.'

Louis didn't like the sound of that. He had the man put down – on the floor – and ordered him to leave, no doubt wishing him an extremely long and healthy life. If it really happened, that is, of course.*

* Though, if I were making this up, I'd have the King say, 'Do you know when I will die?' to which the astrologer would reply, 'Just three days after me.'

Stamp of authority

King George V (1865–1936) loved stamp collecting and his private secretary would often pass on snippets of information or comment on articles relating to stamps. Once, his secretary commented, 'I see in an article in *The Times* today that some damned fool has given £1,400 for a single stamp at a private sale.' 'I am that damned fool,' replied King George.

There is another version of this tale in which His Majesty was the one who commented on the damned fool in *The Times* article before realizing that it was himself!

Top royal

The Margherita pizza was named after Queen Margherita of Savoy (wife of Umberto, King of Italy) in 1889. Created by chef Raffaele Esposito, the pizza was topped with tomatoes, mozzarella cheese and basil, their red, white and green colours representing the three colours of the Italian flag. It became one of the most popular pizza toppings of all time!

Dead rude

In 1669, the famous diarist Samuel Pepys kissed Queen Catherine de Valois on his 36th birthday, even though she'd been dead since 1437. Catherine, wife of Henry V, was buried in Westminster Abbey in the old Lady Chapel but Henry VII had this pulled down and her coffin unceremoniously moved. It was left on bare floorboards near her husband's tomb, but the lid of her coffin was accidentally knocked open . . . and left that way as a tourist attraction for over 200 years. She wasn't given a proper reburial until 1778.

In for a penny

Today's UK currency is (decimal) pounds and pence:

 100 pence = 1 pound sterling.

Before this, the currency was pounds, shillings and pence:

 2 farthings = 1 ha'penny

 2 ha'pennies = 1 penny

 12 pennies = 1 shilling

 20 shillings = 1 pound

 1 pound + 1 shilling = 1 guinea.

(You can see why they changed to decimal, can't you?)

One thing they both have in common is pounds and pennies.

The penny was introduced to England by King Offa (who ruled the kingdom of Mercia from 757 to 796), probably the most powerful Anglo-Saxon king before Alfred the Great.

A 'King Offa Penny' was made of silver, with the words OFFA REX – meaning 'King Offa' – on one side, along with an image of his head.

The highest office

The tallest King of England (so far) was Edward IV (1442–83). He was always described as being very tall and this was confirmed when his coffin was opened in 1789. The skeleton inside was found to be 6 ft 3 in long. That's tall even by today's standards but would have been considered mega-huge in the fifteenth century.

A close second comes another Edward, Edward I (1239–1307) this time, who had the nickname 'Longshanks' and stood 6 ft 2 in tall in his (beautifully) stockinged feet.

It's not clear who the shortest king of England was (when fully grown), though some clever clogs have pointed out that the shortest king – for at least some of his reign – must have been Henry VI (1421–71). Why? Because he was a nine-month-old baby when he became king, and nine-month-old babies are not very tall, even if you can somehow manage to get them to stand up!

A glorious death?

Only two English kings have died in battle. King Harold died at the Battle of Hasting in 1066 – at the hands of William the Conqueror's forces – and Richard III died at the Battle of Bosworth in 1485.

In 1199, Richard I (aka Richard the Lionheart) died while suppressing a revolt in France. One evening, he was strolling around a castle he was besieging when he was shot with a crossbow by someone on the battlements.

A useless surgeon did a very poor job at removing the bolt, and the king's wound became infected. Richard died twelve days later, in his mother's arms: hardly in the heat of battle . . .

The House of Stuart

Nine Stuart monarchs ruled Scotland between 1371 and 1603 and, following King James (Stuart) VI of Scotland also becoming King James I of England in 1603, there were then six Stuart monarchs who held the crown of both countries (with an interruption during the English Civil War between 1649 and 1660).

Although the Stuart King James II was thrown off the throne in 1688, he was replaced by his daughter, Mary II, who ruled with her husband, William, until her death. When William died in 1702, the final Stuart monarch ruled: Mary's sister, Anne.

Queen Anne died without children in 1714, and the British throne passed to the House of Hanover.

The whole Stuart dynasty might well have ended before it began had the first Stuart King, Robert II of Scotland, not survived the fall from a horse that killed his mother. She gave birth to Robert early, as a result of the accident, then died a few hours later.

Psst!

King Abdullah II, King of Jordan (1962–), has been known to disguise himself on a number of different occasions to assess 'the efficiency and levels of bureaucracy' of his government's various departments. His disguises have included a taxi driver, a TV reporter and, in 2001, a white-bearded old man in shabby clothing. He dressed as the bearded old man to visit the tax department in Amman, near his palace, and was accompanied by Prince Ali, his half-brother who was in charge of his security. He mingled with members of the public waiting to file tax returns, fill in forms or make enquiries.

The tax officials only realized that the 'bearded old man' might not be quite what he seemed when he was driven away in a royal motorcade, his car flanked by palace security jeeps, their sirens wailing!

Kings, castles and catastrophe

King Ludwig II of Bavaria (1845–86) love creating fantasy, fairytale castles.* He spent *millions* of pounds on having them built and furnished in the most wildly extravagant way imaginable (which would have cost *billions* today). When the royal coffers were almost empty, he just wanted to keep on spending.

He gained the nickname 'Mad King Ludwig' but this is highly suspect because he was diagnosed in an extremely short space of time by a panel of four psychiatrists who'd never met him. When he was deposed – in other words lost the crown – as a result, he mysteriously died *the very next day*.

On 13 June 1886, at around 6 p.m., he went for a walk along the shores of Lake Starnberg with one of the psychiatrists from the panel by the name of Dr Bernhard von Gudden. When the two men hadn't returned some three hours later, people went looking for them. At around 11.30 p.m. Ludwig and von Gudden

* The most famous of which must be Neuschwanstein Castle in Bavaria, which appears in the film *Chitty Chitty Bang Bang*.

were found floating face-down in the shallow water. The king's watch had stopped at 6.54 p.m.

The official verdict? Suicide. It was strange enough that Ludwig might suddenly decide to take his own life in that way, but Dr von Gudden? What would make a psychiatrist suddenly decide to kill himself at exactly the same time? It was preposterous!

The new king was Ludwig's brother, Otto. The only problem was that he was genuinely, beyond question, mad.

A sporting chance

Prince Willem-Alexander of Orange* (1967–)
once entered the famous 200-kilometre
'Eleven Cities Ice-Skating Marathon' under the
pseudonym W. A. van Buren.** It didn't take
long for him to get recognized so, by the time
he reached the end, both his mother, Queen
Beatrix, and father, Prince Claus, were there to
greet him!

* Crown Prince of the Netherlands/Holland.
** Van Buren being one of the less well known of
his numerous family surnames! (He used the same
surname when entering the New York marathon.)

Buck party

The original front of Buckingham Palace was far less grand than it is today. The new facade, made of 6,000 tons of white Portland stone, was erected with incredible speed. It took about 500 workmen, working day and night, just under three months, in 1913.

By way of a 'Thank you!', King George V (1865–1936) arranged for a meal for the 500* at the Holborn Restaurant. At each man's place was a new clay pipe and packet of strong tobacco bearing the royal coat of arms and the inscription 'From H.M. the King'. According to a contemporary newspaper report, most men pulled out their own tobacco to smoke, saving the king's gift as a souvenir.

The main course was mutton and roast beef, washed down with warm beer to the sounds of an orchestra playing ragtime.

Though the king and queen were 'unable to attend', he sent a message of thanks. All in all, there was plenty of good cheer and shouting of, 'God save the King!'

* Including common labourers, bricklayers, carpenters, hod-carriers, hoisters and stonemasons.

Up in flames

Windsor Castle, the largest inhabited castle in the world, caught fire on Friday, 20 November 1992, when a spotlight set fire to a curtain in the Queen's private chapel, during a period of restoration work.

The alarm was pressed at 11.37 that morning and during the course of the day there were 35 engines and over 250 firefighters tackling the blaze. By 8 p.m. the fire was under control, but pockets of fire kept burning until the following day.

Over a million gallons of water – some direct from the River Thames – were needed to put the fire out.

Members of the royal household saved what could be easily carried between them. The Queen, Prince Charles and Prince Andrew (who was already on the site) all visited the scene. Fortunately, no one died and no one was seriously injured. The dramatic television pictures of the iconic landmark ablaze were beamed around the world.

When the prime minister announced that the government would be paying £50 million for the repair of the castle, there was a public backlash.* Many people thought that it should be the Queen rather than the public who footed the bill. Especially because, unlike all her subjects, the Queen herself didn't pay any income tax, and many very minor royals were also paid for by the public.

In February 1993, the prime minister not only announced that the Queen had offered to pay income tax (which he'd accepted) and declared that in future only she, her husband and her mother** would be paid for out of the public purse, but also that she would pay for 70 per cent of the cost of repairs to the castle, generating additional money by opening parts of Buckingham Palace and Windsor Castle to the paying public.

The restoration work eventually cost around £37.5 million and was completed in under five years.

* The matter was complicated by the fact that technically the castle belongs to the government and not its royal inhabitants.
** The Duke of Edinburgh and Queen Elizabeth, the Queen Mother.

Pleased to meet you, wife

The first time King Charles I met fifteen-year-old Queen Henrietta Maria (1609–69) as his wife was not at their wedding in France, but in Dover. (They'd been married 'by proxy' in France, with someone standing in for the king.) They met soon after her ship had landed from Calais. Henrietta Maria's English was extremely limited, but she'd been practising a few stock phrases to use on his arrival. As it was, she was in the middle of breakfast when he arrived and was so flustered that she forgot her words and burst into tears.

Things apparently improved when he suggested that she might wear high heels to lessen the height difference, and he started studying her feet. She had an attack of the giggles.

They set off for Canterbury for a second wedding (with both of them present this time) in a merry mood.

Queen without a crown

Charles I's wife, Henrietta Maria (1609–69), was Catholic and he was Protestant. For this reason, she absolutely refused to take part in his coronation, because it wasn't a Catholic ceremony. Charles did all he could to try to persuade her, but she wouldn't budge.

Queen Henrietta Maria fled England during the Civil War, so was already in France when Parliament had Charles executed in 1649. She was penniless so, swallowing all her pride, she sent a message to England's new ruler, Oliver Cromwell, asking for some kind of allowance.

Oliver Cromwell sent the message back that she was no true queen of England because she'd refused to be crowned and was, therefore, not entitled to a penny!

'Wise kings generally have wise counsellors;
and he must be a wise man himself who
is capable of distinguishing one.'

Diogenes

The gift of life

The British royal family has been given a wide variety of animals during Queen Elizabeth II's reign. According to the British monarchy's official website, these include:

 1 Syrian brown bear

 various sloths

 1 baby crocodile

 1 canary from Germany

 2 black beavers from Canada

 2 giant turtles from the Seychelles

 1 elephant ('Jumbo') from Cameroon

 and some jaguars from Brazil.

Apparently, the more 'unusual animals' are looked after at London Zoo.

When it came to the crunch

In his book *The Twelve Caesars* (AD 121), the Roman historian Suetonius had much to say about the Emperor Caligula, most of it rather unpleasant. He claimed that Caligula would sometimes shut up the city's grain stores just for the pleasure of knowing people would go hungry. As for his own food bills, when Caligula discovered how much it would cost to feed cattle to the wild beasts he had provided for a gladiatorial show, he decreed that criminals should be eaten instead. Reviewing the line of prisoners (and without examining the charges against them), he selected the victims by simply choosing those who happened to be standing between two bald men – 'from baldhead to baldhead'.

All-new 350-year-old Crown jewels

All that remains of the original British Crown jewels is a gold thirteenth-century Anointing Spoon, the Sword of Temporal Justice, the Sword of Spiritual Justice and the Sword of Mercy. Nothing else survived the destruction ordered by Oliver Cromwell, following King Charles I's execution in 1649. Cromwell wanted to destroy these symbols of kingship. The gems from these earlier Crown jewels were yanked from their settings, then the gold was sent to the (once-Royal) Mint to be melted down, including pieces dating back to the time of Edward the Confessor.

When the monarchy was restored in 1660, King Charles II ordered the making of a whole new set of crowns, orbs, sceptres, rings and the like, forming the basis of today's Crown jewels, though these have been chopped and changed, modified and added to in the centuries since.

Colonel Blood and the Crown jewels

In 1671, a certain Irishman by the name of Colonel Thomas Blood (1617–80) tried to steal the new Crown jewels from the Tower of London (where they're still housed today). The first part of his plan was to befriend Talbot Edwards, 'the Master of the Jewel House', by dressing up as a parson and visiting the Tower with a female accomplice playing the part of his wife.* His 'wife' faked stomach pains, and Edwards helped her. A few days later, Blood – still disguised as a parson – returned with a 'thank you' gift for Edwards for his kindness, and the two men struck up an apparent friendship.

Next, Blood persuaded Edwards to let his 'nephew' and some of his friends have a private viewing of the jewels, after a meal in his apartment at the Tower. Little did the Master of the Jewel House know, but these men were carrying daggers and pistols**.

* At the time it was possible to visit the Tower of London and to see the jewels in return for a small payment to the Master of the Jewel House.
** Some accounts say that they were also carrying swordsticks: harmless-looking walking canes with blades hidden inside them.

They threw a cloak over him and hit him over the head. He was even stabbed a few times.

Blood now flattened out the King Edward's Crown to fit it under his parson's cloak, while an accomplice filed the Sceptre with a Cross in two and stuffed it in his bag. They had to work fast.

As Blood and his gang were about to leave, not only did Talbot Edwards' son, Wythe Edwards, unexpectedly arrive, but the brave Talbot Edwards managed to free himself, shouting, 'Treason! Murder! The crown is stolen!'

With the alarm raised, the thieves fled, dropping the sceptre as they went and firing at the Tower guards, hitting and injuring one of them. Blood was caught by a Captain Beckman and, in the struggle, the squashed crown fell from Blood's parson's cloak. The globe and orb were recovered too, if a bit bashed and with a few precious stones loose or missing.

When it came to questioning Colonel Blood, he refused to answer to anyone but King Charles II himself, and this is where matters took a very strange turn indeed.

Blood had tried to steal the *Crown jewels*. He had attacked and stabbed the Master of the Jewel House. He had fired upon the Tower guards . . . and how did the king punish him?

Execution?

Imprisonment?

Neither. The king pardoned him. In fact, he not only pardoned Colonel Blood, he also gave him land in Ireland which generated the not inconsiderable income of £500 a year. In effect, he *rewarded* the colonel for his bungled robbery.

The question is, of course, why? And the answer may never be known. There are a number of theories ranging from 'The king liked the rogue' or 'He was worried Blood's followers might seek revenge' to 'The king may have planned the theft of the Crown jewels himself, because he was very short of funds'.

This final suggestion may sound preposterous, but it would make sense of why Charles II was so quick to forgive the rapscallion Colonel Blood.

Off with her head!

In 1536, King Henry VIII of England had had enough of his second wife, Anne Boleyn (c.1501–36) so he had her tried and convicted of trumped-up charges, including treason. She was then sentenced to death either by burning at the stake or by being beheaded. Kind man that he was,* Henry chose beheading.

In fairness, Henry didn't leave the job to his usual home-grown executioner. (Beheadings could be botched jobs, taking four or five blows from the axe to remove a head from its body. Why? Because English executioners were more used to hanging people, so weren't experienced with the axe.) Instead, the king had a skilled 'headsman' sent over from France.

On the 19 May 1536, Anne was escorted by 200 Yeomen of the Guard** to the Parade Ground inside the Tower of London. Her hair was 'up' – so that her neck was clearly visible to the headsman – with a white coif*** and small black cap on top. In her hands she

* Joke.
** Better known as Beefeaters.
*** A loose hoodlike cap.

carried a white hanky and a prayer book. A gold cross hung from a chain around her waist.

At the top of the wooden execution platform – called the scaffold – she was met by the executioner dressed in black, with a 'half mask' covering the top of his head and hiding his appearance. Scattered around the floor of the platform was straw (to sop up her blood). Among a pile of this straw, hidden from sight, was the razor-sharp sword he would use (instead of a cumbersome axe) to cut off her head.

Anne made a short speech to the small crowd, which began: 'Good Christian people, I am come hither to die, for according to the law, and by the law, I am judged to die, and therefore I will speak nothing against it. I am come hither to accuse no man, nor to speak anything of that whereof I am accused and condemned to die, but I pray God save the king and send him long to reign over you . . .' and ended with, 'O Lord have mercy on me, to God I commend my soul.' She is said to have spoken with great strength and dignity.

After this, she changed into a white cap, knelt and prayed. From behind her back, the executioner then removed the sword from its hiding place and sliced through the Queen's neck with a single blow.

The late Queen's ladies-in-waiting later recovered the head. It was put with her body in a makeshift coffin made from a box for storing arrows, and was buried within the Tower walls.

A beard innocent of treason

Sir Thomas More (1478–1535) was a long time confidant and one-time Lord Chancellor of King Henry VIII, who – like so many before and after him – eventually fell out with the king (in his case, over religion). He was executed on 6 July 1535, and he seems to have had a lot to say on the matter.

On climbing the steps to the scaffold, he said, 'I pray you, I pray you, Master Lieutenant, see me safe up and for my coming down, let me shift for myself.'

Once up there, he said, 'that he died the king's good servant, but God's first.'

Next, he and his executioner knelt and prayed. As he got to his feet, the executioner asked Sir Thomas for forgiveness. More kissed him, saying, 'Pick up thy spirits, man, and be not afraid to do thine office; my neck is very short, take heed therefore thou strike not awry for having thine honesty.'

He even seems to have had the strength and courage for a little beard humour. Placing his head on the block, he carefully moved his long, flowing beard – which he had grown since his trial – to one side, to escape the executioner's blade. 'For it has committed no treason,' he explained.

Sir Thomas More's head was chopped off and placed on a spike on London Bridge. It was later retrieved by his daughter, Margaret Roper, and in all likelihood buried in the family vault in St Dunstan's Church Canterbury,* possibly even in her own arms when she died, though there are those who believe it to be in Chelsea Old Church, in London.

More was later made a saint.

* About four doors down from where I used to live in St Dunstan's Street.

Sunk without trace

King John's (1167–1216) last days weren't his finest. Famously, he managed to lose the Crown jewels while retreating from a French invasion. The king was travelling from Lincolnshire to Norfolk, when he was taken ill. He decided to go back to Spalding, the long way round (to avoid the unfriendly rebels lurking in East Anglia). Meanwhile, he sent his luggage – including the Crown jewels – the quick way: along a causeway and then across a ford where the Wash met the River Welland. It was very marshy.

This route would have been fine at low tide, but the king's baggage train of horse-drawn wagons was far too heavily laden and slow to avoid the incoming tide. The result? Wagons, frightened horses, weapons and even some knights found themselves sinking in the quicksand-like mud. Much was lost, including the Crown jewels.

When John heard the news, his health took an even bigger turn for the worse. At Swinburne Abbey he was given food and drink but didn't feel welcome. In fact, the story goes, he was *so* suspicious of the monks, he had one of them taste his cider before he'd risk drinking it . . . What he didn't know was that the cider-tasting monk promptly went back to his cell to die in agony, knowing that he'd drunk poison.

The sick and poisoned King John reached Newark, dying in the Bishop of Lincoln's castle there. His nine-year-old son, Henry, was now king.

Virgin territory

Virginia is named after England's Queen Elizabeth I (1533–1603) who – never having married nor had children – was called the Virgin Queen.

The original Virginia* was on the Island of Roanoke off the coast of what is now North Carolina, USA. It was the site of a colony first set up in 1585. (This was only England's second settlement in the New World, the first having failed.) A later colony, set up on Roanoke in 1587, was the site of one of North America's first big mysteries: all the colonists disappeared. They were never seen again.

The name Virginia was used again for the settlement which was to become the State of Virginia. It was founded in 1610. As well as those who chose to start a new life in the New World – and, don't forget, the native population were already living there – many early Virginians were convicts and prisoners of war transported there against their will.

Virginia declared independence from its British rulers on 15 May 1776.

* Named by Sir Walter Raleigh.

289

Getting even

Julius Caesar (c.100–44 BC) was once captured by pirates when he was on the way to Rhodes. This was in the days before he was the incredibly important, incredibly famous, incredibly powerful Julius Caesar, but he *was* from a rich, important family . . . and it was money the pirates were interested in.

They took him ashore and prepared to send out a ransom demand. According to one version of events, his captors were originally going to ask for twenty talents.* When the young Julius heard this, he flew into a terrible rage, insisting that his life was worth much more than that, and they should ask for fifty.

The pirates took his advice. While waiting for the ransom to be paid, they looked after their prisoner well, and even played sports with him. But Caesar warned them that, when the demands were met and he was released, he'd come back, hunt them down and have them tried and executed.

Either the pirates weren't listening or they didn't take him seriously. Instead of clearing

* A silver denomination of currency in the ancient world.

out as soon as the money was paid, they hung around to share it out between them.

This gave Julius the chance to do just as he'd told them he would. The pirates were rounded up in next to no time. They were indeed tried. They were indeed found guilty. They were indeed sentenced to death. The method of death was crucifixion, a slow, lingering death on a cross.

Because the pirates had treated him reasonably when he'd been their prisoner, Caesar had them strangled on their crosses to hasten their deaths . . . which some of you might think was most considerate of him.

A king by any other name

During the Wars of the Roses – an English civil war between the Yorkists and the Lancastrians – Henry VI (1421–71), King of England and head of the Lancastrians, won an important victory at the Battle of St Albans in 1461.

Well, to be fair, his wife Margaret of Anjou actually led the Lancastrian forces to victory. She was a bit of a tough cookie and had earned the nickname 'the She-Wolf of France' because she was a woman, she could be as fierce as a wolf when she wanted to be, and Anjou is in France.

During the battle, Henry himself sat under a tree and watched events unfold in front of him. He had some guards with him. Of course they were there to protect him from any Yorkists who might turn up but, at the same time, they were also there to keep an eye on him. Henry was far from well, having had a number of nervous breakdowns, and was little more than king in name.

As for the Wars of the Roses, they were far from over . . .

'I will be good'

George III's eldest son ruled Britain after him as King George IV. George IV died without any children to inherit the crown so it passed to his surviving brother, who ruled as William IV.* When William died, he had no surviving children either, so the crown passed to the daughter of George III's fourth son, the late Duke of Kent . . .

. . . so it's not as if this young lady – for she inherited the throne when she had just turned eighteen – had been born in the knowledge that she'd one day become queen. It was only as time went on that it became more and more apparent that it could well be a possibility.

When the girl was just ten years old (in 1830) she was looking through a copy of *Howlett's Tables of the Kings and Queens of England*, when she noticed that her governess had updated it, bringing the line of succession – with the latest members of the royal family – up to date.

'I never saw that before,' said the girl.

* George III's third son.

'No, Princess,' responded Baroness Lehzen, her governess. 'It was not thought necessary that you should.'

'I am nearer to the throne than I thought,' she said. 'I will be good.'

The girl was Princess Drina, short for Princess Alexandrina . . . but she ruled for sixty-four years, as one of Britain's best-known monarchs, under the name of Queen Victoria (1819–1901).

Done for

Visit the Scottish palace of Holyrood in Edinburgh and someone may well point out where there was once said to be a stain on the floor where Mary, Queen of Scots's secretary spilt his blood. That would be quite some stain because the palace has been altered and the floors replaced many times since that day in 1566 when David Rizzio was brutally murdered.

He had been sitting having dinner with Mary (1542–87), when the Scottish queen's husband, Lord Darnley, burst into the room with a group of co-conspirators.* Rizzio was dragged away, screaming, 'Save me, lady!' and he even managed to grab hold of the queen's skirts.

He was encouraged to let go of Mary, Queen of Scots, when one of the would-be assassins pointed a pistol at her pregnant belly.

* These included the decidedly ill Lord Ruthven, who had a feverish enough temperature without choosing to wear armour under his cloak.

Pulled from the room, Rizzio was stabbed fifty-six times. His body was then stripped of his fine clothes and jewellery, and thrown down a stairwell.

Although Darnley couldn't actually bring himself to stab Rizzio, his dagger was left at the scene by the other assassins to show that he was a part of the conspiracy.

The exact reason why Rizzio was killed is a little fuzzy. Darnley suspected the man of being his wife's lover, and may well have planned to kill Mary too if it increased his chances of becoming King of Scotland. But there were plots and counterplots too.

And, in the end, Mary and Darnley fled to Dunbar Castle together.

If you want to get ahead . . .

On 14 December 2010, scientists confirmed that a mummified head, in private collections since 1793, was indeed that of King Henri IV of France (1553–1610). Led by the forensic medical examiner* Philippe Charlier of University Hospital R. Poincaré in Garches, France, a team of researchers digitally reconstructed the face and compared this with sculptures and portraits of Henri.** The similarity was remarkable. This, along with matching radiocarbon dating, left the experts in no doubt that this was the king's head. Plans were announced that it would be given a royal burial . . .

It had, of course, been buried before (along with the rest of his body), but had been removed after his tomb was desecrated – along with many others – during the French Revolution, in which France's monarchy was swept away.

* And osteo-archaeologist.
** Who was assassinated in 1610.

297

On the up

'I [would] never again be free to think, speak or act as I really feel I should think, speak and act.' So said Elizabeth Bowes-Lyon (1900–2002) when discussing the problems of accepting the marriage proposal of Prince Albert, the Duke of York.

After three or four proposals, however, she accepted Bertie's proposal and she became the Duchess of York at a marriage ceremony in April 1923.

Despite being a 'Lady', Elizabeth Bowes-Lyon was technically a commoner, and this was the first time since 1660 that a commoner had married such a senior member of the royal family, so she was guaranteed her place in history.

As it was, her role was to become a far more significant one. When Edward VIII gave up the throne to marry the American divorcee Wallis Simpson, it passed to Bertie, Duke of York. He became King George VI. And his wife, the duchess? She became his queen, of course, later Queen Elizabeth the Queen Mother, mother to Queen Elizabeth II.

A moving act

At the wedding of the future King George VI (1895–1952) to his bride, the future Queen Elizabeth,* there was a slight delay in the proceedings. The procession came to a halt when the bride stopped near the entrance to Westminster Abbey. She placed her bridal bouquet of white roses on the Tomb of the Unknown Warrior.** This started a tradition. Since then, every royal bride married in the abbey places a bouquet on the tomb. But she was the first, and others leave the bouquet on their way *back* from the altar rather than on their way to it.

* The Queen Mother (to Queen Elizabeth II).
** She paused to remember one of her brothers who had been killed in the war.

A final, sad goodbye

'I bent over him and said to him, 'Es ist kleines Frauchen' (it is your little wife) and he bowed his head . . . He seemed half dozing, quite quiet . . . I left the room for a moment and sat down on the floor in utter despair. Attempts at consolation from others only made me worse . . . I took his dear left hand which was already cold . . . Two or three long but perfectly gentle breaths were drawn, the hand clasping mine, and (oh! it turns me sick to write it) *all all* was over . . .'

So wrote Queen Victoria (1819–1901) on the death of her beloved husband, Prince Albert. Others in the room included her daughters Princess Alice and Princess Helena, and her eldest boy Bertie, Prince of Wales. The queen partly blamed the prince for Albert's death. It was when Albert went to Cambridge to confront Bertie about his loose morals that he caught the typhoid fever which finally killed him on that fateful December day in 1861.

Out of the ashes

On 25 May 1962 some 2,000 people sat in the ruins of Coventry Cathedral in specially erected stands. In the brand new cathedral alongside sat a further 2,300 people. This was the consecration ceremony for the new cathedral designed by Basil Spence, winner of a competition open to anybody and everybody.

There were twelve archbishops, along with bishops, deans and provosts from every single diocese in Britain, and Queen Elizabeth II (1926–).

This was a particularly significant and moving occasion because it not only marked the dedication and opening of the new cathedral but also acknowledged the night of 14 November 1940. It was on this date that the city of Coventry endured the longest night of bombing on a UK town or city during the whole of the Second World War. Over 500 German bombers dropped wave after wave of high explosive and fire bombs.

As well as the cathedral, over 4,000 homes were destroyed along with three-quarters of the factories. Around 1,000 people were injured and about 600 killed.*

Now a new cathedral had risen out of the ashes, the remains of the previous building left as a reminder of the city's tragic yet defiant history.

* Exact numbers were never established. Some believe that the final death toll may have been nearer 1,000.

This time with feeling

King Henry III (1207–72) was crowned King of England twice. The first crowning had been when he was aged nine, and was a rather hurried affair. His father, King John, died in 1216, and – to avoid any usurpers arguing that the boy was too young to rule – Henry was crowned as quickly as possible in St Peter's Abbey, Gloucester, with only three bishops and a handful of nobles present. In fact, 'crowning' is rather a grand term because Henry's father, King John, had lost the Crown jewels in the Wash. Instead, a simple gold band was placed on the boy's head. The important thing was to get it *done*, not how to do it.

Then, in 1220, there was a far grander coronation in Westminster Abbey, where eight coronations had previously taken place. This time, the all-important Archbishop of Canterbury* did the crown-on-the-head bit. Henry III was a conscientious and religious king, so this second coronation was very significant and important to him, especially because it had been ordered by His Holiness the Pope in person.

* Stephen Langton, the man credited with dividing the Bible into the books, chapters and verses used today.

303

Floral tributes for a foul end

On 21 May each year, representatives from
Eton College, Windsor, and King's College,
Cambridge, come to Wakefield Tower in the
Tower of London and place white flowers –
lilies from Eton, roses from King's College –
on a tablet set in the floor of the oratory.*
This marks the spot where their founder, King
Henry VI (1421–71), is said to have been
murdered.

The details of the death are somewhat sketchy.
No one is even sure who actually carried out
the crime, though the usual suspects include
Richard, Duke of Gloucester.**

Henry VI is said to have been brutally
murdered when kneeling at prayer. He had
been imprisoned in the Tower following the
defeat of his Lancastrian forces at the Battle of
Tewkesbury (by the Yorkist ruling as Edward
IV).

* Prayer room.
** Later King Richard III.

304

There is also a tradition of laying flowers in St George's Chapel, Windsor, on the evening of 20 May. Here, in addition to white lilies and roses, the Henry VI Society now lays yellow roses. This symbolizes the awarding of the 'Papal Golden Rose' to Henry VI by Pope Eugenius IV for his 'services to religion'.

Sticky ends

During the Wars of the Roses, the Yorkists fought the Lancastrians for the English throne. Though Henry VI was still alive and still technically king, that didn't stop Edward, Duke of York (1442–83), trying to rule as Edward IV. The Battle of Tewkesbury in 1471 was a defining moment in Edward's plan to be the one and only king. He was victorious, defeating the Lancastrian forces.

Immediately after the battle, he's said to have come face to face with another Edward. This was Henry's seventeen-year-old son, the Prince of Wales. According to this version of events, when asked by Edward of York why he dared to oppose him, the young Lancastrian replied, 'To recover my father's crown and mine own inheritance.'

Edward of York then slapped him across the face with his gauntlet.* This would have been painful enough but was only a signal for something far more painful to come. Edward's guards promptly dragged the young Prince of Wales away and stabbed him.

* Metal glove.

To death.

The prince's father, Henry, fared no better. Having been taken prisoner, he was put in the Tower of London, and was murdered just a few months later.

Hide and hide (again)

While on the run from Roundhead forces, King Charles II of England (1630–85) hid in many places, most famously an oak tree,* which included the homes of Royalists, a priest's hole,** a barn, a pub or two, and even among the ancient standing stones of Stonehenge on Salisbury Plain.

* Thereafter referred to as 'the royal oak'.
** A priest's hole was a (usually small and cramped) hiding place for a priest in the home of a Catholic family's home, built at the time when Roman Catholics were persecuted.

When hiding in the home of Francis Wyndham near Yeovil, Somerset (in September 1651), he witnessed the local villagers in the middle of some kind of celebration. When enquiring what it was, he was informed that they were celebrating the death of young King Charles at the Battle of Worcester at the beginning of the month. (Not to be confused with the old King Charles – his father – who'd had his head chopped off in 1649.) It was in the king's interests not to tell them that they were mistaken and that he was very much alive and well!

On 15 October, Charles managed to board a brig* named *Surprise*, which was pretending to sail to the Isle of Wight but, once out to sea, changed from its plotted course and, the following morning, landed the king in France. His mother was waiting to greet him.

* A two-masted square-rigged sailing vessel.

Dressing up a claim

Charles Edward Stuart's grandfather was King James II of England and James VII of Scotland so, after his father, he might well have expected to become king one day too. As it was, Catholic James II was thrown off the throne and replaced by Protestant monarchs William and Mary. This meant that Charles's father, James Francis Edward Stuart, was in the position of being a pretender: someone claiming the right to the throne but not officially recognized as such. (And, of course, those who'd booted James out weren't about to recognize his descendants' perfectly legitimate rights!)

Over time, James Francis Edward Stuart (1688–1766) became known as the 'Old Pretender' and Charles Edward Stuart (1720-88) as the 'Young Pretender'. Charles also gained the nickname 'Bonnie Prince Charlie'.

In 1745, it was Bonnie Prince Charlie who tried to lead an uprising to put a Stuart – in other words *himself* – back on the throne, with the help of Scottish forces. This was the Jacobite Rebellion, and it ended in disaster for him. His best bet was to flee the country;

something made all the harder by the big
reward offered for his capture, dead or alive.
It's harder to trust people when you have a
price on your head.

There's a famous account of Charles being
rowed to the Isle of Skye by one Flora
MacDonald, disguised as her female servant
Betty Burke. There was even a popular song
written about it, with the lines:

> *Speed, bonnie boat,*
> *Like a bird on the wing,*
> *'Onward!' the sailors cry.*
> *Carry the lad that was born to be King,*
> *Over the sea to Skye.*

Less well-known is his return from Skye,
dressed as a manservant this time. He called
himself 'Lewie Caw' and covered his head in
bandages, pretending he had a sore face!!!

Back on mainland Scotland, he befriended
a group of Scots – on the run since their
defeat at the Battle of Culloden – who became
known as 'the seven men of Glenmoriston'.
They swore to protect 'their king', hiding out
together in the wild moorland, sleeping in
a cave.

After five months of dodging English troops, Bonnie Prince Charlie finally made it to France before eventually returning to Italy, where he'd been born.

All attempts by the Stuarts to claim the throne were at an end.

I swear by Almighty God!

Today we refer to people who wilfully destroy property as vandals, after an east German tribe called the Vandals who caused the ancient Romans *real* bother.* We talk about people 'going berserk' if they get violently angry. That term comes from the Berserkers, a group of Norse warriors who fought in an uncontrollable trance-like rage . . .

. . . but when the fifteenth-century French talked about 'the Goddons' it referred very specifically to English soldiers, and wasn't in reference to the fierceness of their fighting prowess, despite the English having famously beaten them at the Battle of Agincourt.

The term came about after the battle of 1415, when the English King Henry V (1387–1422) laid siege to the city of Rouen, capital of Normandy, for six months (from July 1418 to January 1419). Its citizens died in huge numbers from disease and starvation, resorting to eating rats and the weeds between paving stones. Outside the city walls, Henry's

* They even sacked Rome (not as in 'You're fired!', but as in 'to capture, loot and pillage').

troops kept up the pressure by capturing and killing anyone they could find, stringing up the corpses in full view of those within.

So why 'Goddons'? What did it *mean*?

As well as having to witness the English soldiers' cruelty, the besieged French also had to endure their endless swearing. 'Goddon' is a corruption of the words 'God damn'!

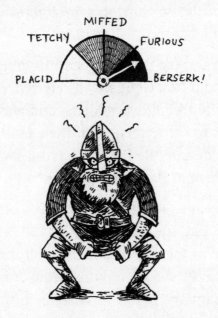

This doesn't quite fit with the images the English had back home of good King Henry and his fine fighting force!

Revenge at last

Although Henry III was technically King of England, there was a period during his reign when the real power lay with French-born Simon de Montfort, Earl of Leicester (c.1208–65), and the barons. All this was to change in 1265 at the Battle of Evesham. Henry III was actually de Montfort's prisoner at the time so, rather confusingly, was actually dressed in de Montfort's colours.

The royalist troops far outnumbered de Montfort's by two to one, and proudly wore red crosses to show that – in their opinion – God was on their side! They were led by Henry's son, Prince Edward* (1239–1307). Not only were his forces defeated, but many of the barons themselves were killed, including Simon de Montfort.

In those days, it was more usual for barons to be taken prisoner and ransomed rather than killed. Death was what more commonly happened to ordinary soldiers. But not on this day. There were many scores to settle. One commentator described it as 'an episode of

* Later king Edward I, Edward Longshanks and Hammer of the Scots.

noble bloodletting unprecedented since the [Norman] Conquest' and as 'the end of the age of chivalry'.

It was lucky for Henry III that he was recognized, despite being in de Montfort's colours, or he might have been killed for being an enemy of himself, the king!

Once dead, de Montfort's hands, feet and head were hacked off. The head was awarded to Edward's loyal supporter, Roger Mortimer, who had fought long and hard beside him. He sent it home as a present to his wife!

Up in smoke

Pope Urban VII (1521–90), born Giovanni Battista Castagna, was pope for less than two weeks in September 1590. His papacy lasted twelve days, to be precise, making it the shortest reign in the history of the papacy (so far). He died* before he was even crowned. Despite his being on the papal throne for less than a fortnight, he still managed to introduce an extremely memorable papal decree: possibly the world's first public smoking ban. What's more, it had the backing of God's Representative On Earth (so carried more weight than, for example, an up-to-£200-fine sticker on a train window). Urban threatened to excommunicate anyone who 'took tobacco inside a church, whether it be by chewing, smoking or sniffing.'

* Probably of malaria. He left 30,000 scudi (which was a lot of money) to be shared among poor girls as part as their dowry when they married.

Entitled to a title?

Once in power, Emperor Napoleon (1769–1821) never forgot his family. He gave out titles and honours like confetti. With the French empire stretching right across Europe, he now had some really *important* titles to give out: kingships and the like.

Napoleon made his elder brother, Joseph, King of Naples; he made brother Louis King of Holland; brother Jerome King of Westphalia;* sister Caroline Grand Duchess of Berg and, later, also Queen of Naples; and sister Elisa, he made Grand Duchess of Tuscany.

He offered the role of King of Spain to his brother Lucien, but Lucien turned it down. (This had something to do with the fact that Napoleon really didn't like Lucien's wife and kept on urging him to ditch her and to marry someone else. Lucien, on the other hand, was very fond of his wife, thank you very much, so moved to Italy with her to retire.)

So Napoleon ended up making Joseph – already King of Naples, remember – the King of Spain too!

* A state in Prussia, now a part of Germany.

Say it with treasure

In 1581, Francis Drake arrived at Deptford, London, in his famous ship, the *Golden Hind*. He was met by Queen Elizabeth I, who came on board for a mighty banquet. It was here, on the quarterdeck, that she knighted him.* But why such a right royal welcome? Why such an honour? Because although Drake had been away for three years, Deptford wasn't his first stop on his return.

A few days previously, he'd landed off Plymouth and sent word to Elizabeth. He had managed to acquire a 'vast treasure' in the Queen's name – mainly through officially approved piracy – and he wanted to know what she'd have him do with it!

Elizabeth was, of course, *delighted* at the news. So delighted, in fact, that she said he could keep the not inconsiderable – all right, the huge – sum of £10,000, but must bring the rest to her in London as soon as possible . . .

. . . hence his arrival in Deptford, and such a warm welcome from his queen.

Nothing gets you in a monarch's good books like the gift of a vast fortune!

* Making him *Sir* Francis Drake.

319

Face it

Between the creation of the effigy* of
Queen Elizabeth I (1533–1603) for her tomb
in Westminster Abbey and that of Queen
Victoria (1819–1901) for her tomb in the
Royal Mausoleum, Frogmore, there wasn't a
single effigy made for the tomb of an English
king or queen: a period of almost 300 years.
Before Elizabeth, such effigies were common,
but none was made for a Stuart monarch
and, although Sir Christopher Wren himself
designed an ornate monument for William
and Mary, it was never actually built.

* A representation of a person, such as a carving or
statue.

In a jam

In 1396, Richard II of England (1367–1400) returned from France with his new bride, Isabella, the seven-year-old eldest daughter of the 'mad' French king, Charles VI. This was Richard's second marriage and it was solemnized in Calais before their departure for England.

The royal couple arrived in Blackheath, then stayed in Kennington for a few days before heading for the Tower of London. By now, news of their arrival had spread across London, causing much excitement.

London Bridge became so crowded with eager onlookers that nine people were crushed to death, 'of whom the Prior of the Austin Canons at Tiptree was one and a worshipful matron of Cornhill was another.'

Sign of the times

According to the events portrayed in the Bayeux Tapestry, a shooting star appeared in the sky during the coronation of King Harold of England (c.1022–66) in 1066, and was seen as a bad omen.

Interestingly, astronomers have calculated that Halley's Comet did, genuinely, appear in the sky in 1066, but not until *long* after the date of Harold's coronation . . .

. . . and, not only that, comets were usually seen as omens of *good* luck.

This really was a case of not letting the facts get in the way of a good story.

Brainy Bess

Princess Elizabeth (1533–1603), later Queen Elizabeth I, was not brought up in the royal household, her mother, Anne Boleyn having been beheaded on the orders of her father, King Henry VIII.

When Elizabeth was just six years old, it was reported that – even if she never had another lesson in her life – her knowledge would be a credit to the king. Elizabeth's tutor, the scholar Roger Ascham, went so far as to say that the princess's mind had 'no womanly weakness, her perseverance is equal to that of a man'. This would have been meant as a compliment in those days, and Elizabeth would certainly have taken it as such.

When Elizabeth was just eleven years old, she translated an entire book from French into English and bound it in a cover she'd embroidered herself. She presented it to her final stepmother, Catherine Parr.

In the last years of the king's life, he had his son Edward – Elizabeth's half-brother – educated alongside her at Hatfield House in Hertfordshire. It's unlikely that anyone ever dreamed that one day she'd end up not only as Queen of England but also as one of its best-remembered monarchs.

Behind the mask

Queen Elizabeth I (1533–1603) knew that her public image was all-important. She was a woman in a man's world and had no intention of marrying and losing grip on her power. It was therefore very important to her as to how she was perceived by others. Hence the 'mask of beauty'.

The mask of beauty was a template – a fixed pattern – which had to be followed by every single artist who drew or painted her. They could not paint her as they truly saw her – for better or for worse – but as the template dictated.

Today, this would be along the lines of only allowing official photographs to be issued and having them retouched/digitally enhanced/Photoshopped before being given the royal seal of approval.

In this way, Elizabeth ensured that the face she presented to the world of people who never actually got to meet her was one of regality, authority and beauty.

Who? What?

Mary Stuart (1542–87), later Mary, Queen of Scots, was born in Scotland but in 1548 it was decided that she should travel to France to be brought up in the French court (because she was to marry the French king's son). To make matters suitably confusing, she travelled on board ship with what were known as the 'Four Maries'. They were:

 Mary Beaton (a distant relative of the influential Cardinal Beaton)

Mary Livingston* (a relation of the all-important Lord Livingston**)

Mary Fleming (said to have 'royal Scottish blood')

Mary Seton (daughter of a lady-in-waiting to Mary Stuart's own mother).

Plus Mary Stuart herself, of course. I wonder if they used nicknames?

* Without an 'e' on the end.
** Without an 'e' on the end.

The visitor beneath the bed

One evening, when retiring to her bedchamber in Holyrood Palace, Edinburgh, Mary, Queen of Scots (1542–87), discovered an uninvited Frenchman hiding under her bed. He was known to her, not least because he was a poet in the royal party who'd accompanied Mary from France to Scotland. His name was Pierre de Châtelard, and he'd already declared undying love for Her Majesty on more than one occasion. He'd been tolerated as a harmless flirt (in truth, the queen seemed to rather like the attention). But this time he'd gone too far. He was forcibly removed.*

* This became the subject of a painting with the poet emerging from beneath a huge four-poster bed not only to startle Mary, Queen of Scots, but also various ladies-in-waiting and her dog (possibly the one which hid under her skirt when she was executed some years later. Or not).

Mary then travelled to Rossend Castle. Once settled, who should burst into her room again than de Châtelard! This time she was actually in the process of undressing, and he tried to embrace her. Mary called for her half-brother, the Earl of Moray, to stab the man. Instead, the poet was dragged off again, but this time he was tried in public (in St Andrews), found guilty, and executed.

The poet once described Mary as 'the most beautiful and most cruel princess of the world'.

As Caesar never said . . .

England's defeat of the Catholic Spanish Armada* in 1588, during the reign of Queen Elizabeth I, went down very well in Protestant Holland. The Dutch even struck a special commemorative medal to mark this glorious victory. It included a picture of the Armada, along with a variation of Julius Caesar's famous words, 'I came, I saw, I conquered.'

This time it read: 'It came, it saw, it fled.'

* A large fleet of ships.

A flight of stairs, a she-wolf – but *no* lettuce

Robert Dudley, Earl of Leicester (*c.*1533–88), either loved Queen Elizabeth I or wanted to marry her in the hope of becoming King of England. Either way, there was a slight problem: he was already married. Luckily for him, this potential barrier – his wife, Lady Dudley – ended up dead at the bottom of the stairs.

Despite this – and rumours were soon flying that (surprise, surprise) Dudley had either pushed his wife or had her pushed – he and Elizabeth never wed.

In the end, he married a woman by the name of Lettice.* Not that Elizabeth called her that. She gave her love-rival the nickname 'she-wolf.'

---

* Not to be confused with 'lettuce', Lettice's maiden name was the wonderfully weird-sounding Lettice Knollys.

But I don't wanna be queen!

Lady Jane Grey (1537–54) was fifteen years old when she became 'queen' for just nine days in July 1553. She had her sixteenth birthday in the Tower of London and was then executed.

Lady Jane Grey was declared queen by John Dudley, Duke of Northumberland, after the death of her second cousin, King Edward VI.* She hadn't expected the crown and she didn't want it. 'The crown is not my right and pleaseth me not,' she said. Even if she'd stayed on the throne longer, she'd only have been a figurehead while others – in other words, Northumberland – ruled 'on her behalf' and for their own ends. 'The Lady Mary is the rightful heir,' she argued, referring to Mary Tudor who – sure enough – became Queen when Jane Grey's nine days were up.

* Her great-grandfather was Henry VII.

Ironically, had Edward VI not died, he and Jane may well have married. As it was, when he realized the young king was dying, Northumberland made Edward promise the crown to Lady Jane, then promptly made her marry his own son, lining him up for some kingly or prince-consort role. The whole thing was wrapped up in the guise of ensuring that the English crown remained in Protestant hands.

The plan failed. Northumberland was executed immediately, Lady Jane within six months, and the Catholic Mary Tudor became Queen Mary I, better known as Bloody Mary. She is best remembered for having around 300 religious dissenters – non-Catholics – burned at the stake.

Burn it!

Queen Matilda* (1102–67) had been promised the throne of England by her father Henry I but, when he died, his nephew Stephen took it, becoming what is generally agreed to be one of England's worst kings. Matilda wanted what she believed to be rightfully hers and there followed many years of civil war.

The Bishop of Winchester, Henri of Blois, was Stephen's brother but, despite this, switched sides and supported her. It was he who declared her queen in February 1141. The trouble was, she turned out to be so high and mighty and arrogant that she very quickly became wildly unpopular. Henri regretted what he'd done and switched his allegiance back to his brother . . .

* She was never crowned and is sometimes referred to as Empress Matilda or 'Domina', but she was queen in everything but name.

. . . so when Matilda set herself up in his own city of Winchester, he wanted her out of there at all costs. He took the rather drastic action of setting fire to the city (conducting operations from his castle on the safety of the outskirts). Winchester burned for six whole weeks, destroying everything from humble dwellings to royal palaces to monasteries to churches.

When Stephen's troops finally arrived, Matilda and her forces had well and truly had enough. They fled, many famously stripping off their armour and pretending to be locals when stopped and questioned.

Matilda's short-lived reign lasted less than nine months.

Dedication to duty

Eadwig the Fair* (c.941–59) is best remembered for missing much of his own coronation banquet. He was crowned at Kingston-upon-Thames in 955, after which a great feast was held to celebrate the occasion . . . only he was more interested in spending time with his girlfriend, so slipped away.

This enraged Dunstan,** Abbot of Glastonbury, who went and found him, stuck his crown back on his head, and dragged him back to the proceedings, embarrassing the new king in front of the nobles.

This led to a serious feud between the two men, with Dunstan fleeing in fear for his life. The girlfriend had become Eadwig's queen!

* Sometimes known as Edwy – but never as Earwig.
** Later Saint Dunstan (after which the street in Canterbury where I used to live was named).

335

Sew, sew, quick, quick, sew

*La Tapisserie de la Reine Matilde,** or the Bayeux Tapestry, as it's known in England, isn't actually a tapestry. Tapestries are made on weaving machines called looms. It's a piece of embroidery, about 230 ft long, all of it sewn by hand. Because it was first known as Queen Matilda's Tapestry, it was assumed by historians that Matilda – William the Conqueror's wife – designed and maybe even sewed it herself. We now know that it was made on the instructions of William's half-brother Odo, Bishop of Bayeux, by a team of women.

* 'Queen Matilda's Tapestry'.

David and Goliath

To call the Battle of Poitiers in 1356 an English triumph against all odds would be an understatement. Edward the Black Prince* (1330–76), son of King Edward III, led a force of 7,000 against French forces numbering as many as 30,000, yet the English still managed to take many thousands of French prisoner, including the King of France himself!

Immediately after the battle, the Black Prince treated King John of France with great respect, waiting on him at table. But His Majesty was a valuable prisoner: he was worth 3 million – yes, 3,000,000 – gold pieces . . . though it did take the French *four years* to cough up. In the meantime, he was kept in chambers at Windsor.

The Black Prince was only twenty-six** at the time of this incredible victory. Tragically, he died just before his forty-sixth birthday, a year before his father.***

* Named after the black armour he loved to wear.
** He was only sixteen when he fought at an earlier famous English victory, the Battle of Crécy.
*** The Black Prince's son became King Richard II on the death of Edward III.

The stuff of legends

In the fifteenth century, the legend of King Arthur was a potent force, and King Henry VII (1457–1509) wanted to be a part of it. Born in Wales, he wanted his right to sit on the English throne to be as strong as possible . . . and, conveniently, his royal genealogists managed to trace his ancestry back to King Arthur himself! They also identified Winchester Castle – in the city of Winchester, ancient capital of England – as Arthur's fabled castle of Camelot.

Henry made sure that he and his wife, Queen Elizabeth of York, were in Winchester for the birth of their first child. It was a boy. The christening at Winchester Cathedral was an incredibly extravagant and opulent affair. The prince was called – you guessed it – Arthur.

Tragically, he never inherited the throne from his father. Arthur died when he was just fifteen. His brother became king instead, and a very famous one at that: Henry VIII. Prince Henry ended up marrying Arthur's widow, Catherine of Aragon, the first of his six wives.

For the glory of God

As well as having the all-important Westminster Abbey enlarged, King Henry III of England (1207–72) showed a lifelong interest in the building of Salisbury Cathedral. It had been begun in 1220, when he was just thirteen years old.

In January 1227, Henry granted a charter turning the settlement of New Sarum, which had sprung up around the building, into the city of Salisbury. He was also present – as guest of honour, I'd imagine – at the consecration of the completed cathedral in 1258.

In between times, he had regularly ridden out from his nearby hunting palace in Clarendon Forest to see how the building work was developing. He also provided practical support. Literally. He supplied the massive timbers holding up the roof.

It was originally assumed that the roof timbers came from wood from Clarendon Forest, but tests in 2003 revealed that the forty or so trees were actually felled in the Dublin area of Ireland, and shipped to England. (The region had recently been conquered by the English.)

Although the main body of the cathedral was completed and consecrated in 1258, the cloisters and Chapter House were not added until 1280, and the tower in 1313, to which the spire was then added. From the ground to the tip of the spire is some 404 ft. It was the tallest human-made structure in the medieval world, apart from the ancient Egyptian pyramids a long, long way away.

Swings and roundabouts

Elizabeth of York (1466–1503) led an extraordinary life, even by the weird and wonderful standards of medieval monarchs. She was one of the ten children of King Edward IV, whose lives were made so hellish by her uncle Richard. He robbed her family of its authority and possessions and at one stage they were living in political asylum. (She had to help her mother, the ex-queen Elizabeth Woodville, raise her nine brothers and sisters.) Uncle Richard became King Richard III when two of Elizabeth's brothers mysteriously 'disappeared' from the Tower of London.*

Fortunately for Elizabeth, Richard was eventually defeated by Henry Tudor from Wales. The same Henry Tudor who became Henry VII and married her.

The tables had been turned once more. Elizabeth of York was now Queen of England.

* One of whom was King Edward V and, technically, reigned for just over three months in 1483, though he was basically his uncle's prisoner for that time.

341

Being ever so 'umble

In July 1483, Richard, Duke of Gloucester (1452–85), had himself crowned King Richard III, following the convenient disappearance of his brother's son.* To show just how humble and God-fearing and righteous he was – and not at all the kinda guy who'd murder his own nephew – he and his wife, Anne of Warwick, walked barefoot from Westminster Hall to Westminster Abbey. Here the pair then stripped to the waist and were anointed with holy oil.

* His brother was Edward IV; his brother's son was (for three months) Edward V.

Cross-pollination

You'll have found that the Wars of the Roses get quite a few mentions in this book. But what were they? Well – and thank you for asking* – the royal house** of the Plantagenets was made up of two rival families: the houses of Lancaster and of York. The Lancastrian emblem was a red rose. The Yorkists' was a white one. And they fought for power. They fought for the throne of England. The battles in this civil war were fought in fits and starts between 1455 and 1485.

The final war was eventually won by the Lancastrian Henry Tudor (1457–1509),*** who – in a very clever move of political astuteness and reconciliation – married Elizabeth of York, daughter of the late King Edward IV. Now there was a Lancastrian king and a Yorkist queen on the throne, and they created the Tudor dynasty. There was a Tudor on the throne for over a hundred years.

* What do you mean you didn't?!
** That's 'house' as in 'family'.
*** Who ruled as Henry VII.

The pud is back!

King George I of England (a German by birth) had only been in England a few months when Christmas 1714 came around, and he insisted that the festivities include Christmas pudding. This would have come as no surprise to those who knew George. He was a big man with a big appetite.

The Christmas pud had been traditional Christmas fare in England in the past but – like so many things pleasurable and connected to Christmas – had been banned or suppressed by Oliver Cromwell's Puritans.

Even after the Restoration (when the Parliamentarians were defeated and King Charles II was on the throne) the Christmas pudding didn't regain its former importance . . .

. . . until George made it the fashionable thing to serve up on your Christmas table. It was back with a vengeance and here to stay. And George? He was even nicknamed 'The Pudding King'.

You must be joking!

King Henry VIII (1491–1547) had a number of court jesters, but Will Sommers is the most famous by far. He was presented to the king at Greenwich in 1525.

And he made the king laugh.

Henry offered him a place in the royal court then and there. Will soon became a firm favourite and was well paid for his services. Later in the king's life, when the ulcers on his legs became a constant pain, it's said that only Sommers could take his mind off them.

As a jester, Sommers was allowed to say things – regardless of a person's rank – that other people (even dukes and earls) could never get away with. He even teased the pompous, self-important (and potentially very dangerous) Cardinal Wolsey, Henry's Lord Chancellor.

Sommers once threw milk in a juggler's face! He did, however, overstep the mark when daring a courtier to say rude things about the queen and a princess . . . resulting in Henry threatening to kill him with his bare hands!

But he was soon forgiven, and actually outlived His Majesty.

Non-king kings

Burger King* is neither a real king nor a burger, but a chain of fast-food burger joints. King Cotton isn't a king-as-in-person either, but refers to the cotton crop which was at the heart of North America's industry . . . in the same way that King Coal refers to coal – the black stuff – but not Old King Cole,** who was a merry old soul (but only in the mythical sense). Elvis Presley*** was the King of Rock'n'Roll, according to Elvis fans, and Nat King Cole**** was simply one of the greatest singers in the history of the world, according to me.*****

* Born Insta-Burger King in 1953, the chain became Burger King in 1955 and has changed hands a number of times since.
** Possibly based on one of three real kings: Coel the Magnificent, Coel the Old, or St Ceneu ap Coel.
*** (1935–77).
**** Born Nathaniel Adams Coles (1919–65).
***** So it must be true.

The singeing of the king's beard

The king who had his beard singed was none other than the mighty King Philip II of Spain (1527–98). But this was a metaphorical singeing rather than an actual one: in other words, his beard wasn't actually lightly burned . . . or even *badly* burned, come to that. But Philip did endure something as painful and embarrassing, and it had to do with those pesky English, during the reign of Elizabeth I.

England was a big thorn in Spain's side. England was Protestant. Spain was Catholic. Henry VIII's first wife had been Spanish. The Queen of England's mother was the woman Henry had ditched his Spanish wife for . . . so there was no love lost between the two seafaring nations.

English privateers (semi-official pirates) kept on attacking Spanish territories and ships in the Indies, stealing large amounts of treasure – enough to affect the Spanish economy!

King Philip had had *enough*. He planned to invade England to put a stop to these attacks, and to turn it back into a Catholic

country (which it had been before Henry VIII broke away from the Church, and the current queen, his daughter Queen Elizabeth I, was excommunicated by the Pope). After all, King Philip had previously been King of England, as well as Spain, during his marriage to Mary I ('Bloody Mary'). But the English had other ideas.

Queen Elizabeth instructed Sir Francis Drake to keep an eye on Spanish preparations for invasion and to frustrate them as much as possible by attacking shipping, supplies, and even ports when possible.

In 1587 King Philip had a large invasion fleet gathered in the bay of Cadiz. In sailed Sir Francis and his fleet, guns blazing, eventually destroying thirty-seven ships* and sailing off with four Spanish ships laden with provisions. Over a hundred Spaniards were killed during the engagement but not one English life was lost.

Drake's forces then sailed along the Spanish and Portuguese coast, attacking more Spanish shipping as they went. They returned to England victorious.

The king of Spain's beard had been well and truly singed.

But why describe the whole incident as a 'singed beard'? Why not as a 'body blow'? Because to singe a beard would be an embarrassment – a loss of face – but not crippling. A singed beard could grow back as good as new – as did King Philip's fleet.

In 1588, the Spanish Armada set sail. Its mission: to invade England.

* According to him. The Spanish said twenty-four.

Taking it on the chin

In Ancient Egypt, beards were considered to be sacred. They were a divine symbol of the gods, so the only living beings who could 'wear' beards were the pharaohs – kings and (some) queens – because they were thought to be gods themselves.

In carvings, painting, statues and hieroglyphs,* pharaohs are depicted with long, thin, tightly plaited, tightly knotted beards. Ancient Egyptian kings and queens would therefore often wear false beards during public ceremonies (hooked in place behind their ears).

These false beards are so un-beard-like to modern eyes that nowadays many people don't realize that they're supposed to *be* beards.

* Ancient Egyptian writing, using thousands of picture symbols.

Turning the tables

Irishman Johannes Scottus Eriugena (c. AD 815–77) – better known as plain old Eriugena – was a well-known Greek scholar, philosopher and theologian, and was thought by many to be one of the most original thinkers in the Middle Ages. He was well respected in continental Europe as well as in his home country and in England.

Once, when dining in the French court, the French king is said to have leaned across the table and asked, 'What separates a drunkard from an Irishman?' This was as much a play on words as a jokey insult to the Irish, because the king phrased the question in Latin – *Quid distat inter sottum et Scottum?* – where *sottum* means 'drunkard'* and *Scottum* means 'Irishman'.**

'What separates a drunkard from an Irishman?' As quick as a flash, Eriugena looked at the king across the table from him and replied: *Mensa tantum*. 'Only a table.'

Fortunately, the king found this funny!

* Or 'sot'.
** Though I bet you'd have thought it meant 'Scotsman'.

352

Full queen ahead!

Queen Elizabeth II (1926–) seems to enjoy riding on miniature steam trains. On more than one occasion she has been driven around the track in Exbury Gardens by fellow steam-enthusiast (and merchant banker) Leopold de Rothschild (who lived in a stately home in the New Forest). In May 2008 – after a private naming ceremony for Rothschild's latest miniature steam engine, the royal blue, five-tonne *Mariloo** – the Queen joined other paying visitors on the half-mile trip around the grounds. Aged eighty-two, she disguised herself in raincoat, headscarf and glasses and no one seemed to recognize her!

* Named after his mother.

Are you pro or anti anti-kings?

In the Holy Roman Empire, as well as the reigning monarchs there was a time when there were anti-kings too. Anti-kings tried to rule in opposition to – and despite – the official emperors. Despite its name, the Holy Roman Empire:

1. wasn't very holy;

2. wasn't very Roman;

3. wasn't really an empire.

It did last for around a thousand years but for much of the time was more of a loose affiliation of territories. At its head was an emperor but as time went on his power lessened while the princes' power increased . . . and then there were these irritating anti-kings who were issuing orders and making laws of their own.

Some anti-kings eventually ended up as officially recognized full-blown emperors, such as Frederick II (1194–1250) . . . who then had to put up with TWO anti-kings 'ruling' in opposition to him!

Stands to reason

Frederick II (1194–1250), Emperor of the Holy Roman Empire, was known as 'The Astonishment' because his behaviour seemed so astonishing to the people of the day! Whether Jew, Christian or Moslem, religion was at the heart of people's lives . . . yet here was a ruler who's said to have declared Moses, Jesus and Muhammad as the 'frauds and deceivers of mankind'.

To be a non-believer at the time was unusual; to express it so openly was virtually unheard of. Because to him all religions were equally unlikely, he showed great religious tolerance – with a few notable exceptions – and happily employed Jewish scholars in a Christian-based society which disapproved of such things.

Frederick's premise was a straightforward one: things needed to be explained by reason. If they couldn't be explained in such a way – if one needed faith to believe in them, rather than facts – then he simply didn't believe.

He even went so far as to ban 'trials by ordeal'. Such trials were legally binding fights based on the principle that God would be on the side of the righteous and make him the winner. Frederick was convinced that it had nothing to do with innocence or guilt, or God being on one's side. The stronger would always win!

Not surprisingly, such views meant he was in constant opposition to various popes and the Catholic Church, and much of his reign was taken up battling with them.

Despite such a logical, scientific mind, Emperor Frederick II was also a patron of the arts and a lover of poetry.

Beardy business

Whereas the young Edward VII is remembered for pulling one of his tutor's beards (as well as throwing stones at him), Queen Elizabeth II is remembered for pulling her grandfather's beard; the difference being that she was a toddler, and her grandfather – George V – was having fun!

Edward VII's father was the perfectionist Prince Albert, who subjected his eldest son – from the age of seven – to an extraordinarily strict regime, involving rigorous exercise and six hours of study a day, six days a week. Little wonder he rebelled.

Elizabeth (Edward's great-granddaughter), on the other hand, spent the first ten years of her life with no inkling that one day she would be queen. She was George V's 'Lilibet' and he was her 'Grandpa England'.

Bless 'em all

When George I came over to England in 1714 to take up the crown – he was a great-grandson of James I – he brought a large entourage with him, which was only to be expected. As well as the usual servants, attendants and secretaries, he brought two eye-catching girlfriends with him. And why did they attract so much attention?

Firstly, there was the well-known fact that he'd left behind his wife, Princess Sophia Dorothea, locked up in a castle (accused, of all things, of adultery). Then there was the appearance of the two ladies. Sophia von Kielmansegg was very large, so was promptly nicknamed 'The Elephant', and, being very tall and thin, Ehrengard Melusine von Schulenburg became know as 'The Maypole'.

Even the prime minister, Robert Walpole, had some rather rude things to say about them!

Leading from the front

At the Battle of Dettingen in Bavaria, in 1743, the combined British, Hanoverian and Hessian forces were led by a fifty-nine-year-old German. He famously rallied his troops into battle with the cry of: 'Don't tell me of danger . . . Fire and behave brave and the French will run!' And the French did, indeed, run. At one stage, his horse bolted but was stopped by a young ensign, who was promoted as a result. The German was none other than Britain's King George II (1683–1820), and he was the last reigning English monarch to lead his troops into battle. Interestingly, England and France had yet to officially declare war!

359

Wrong-footed

How William the Conqueror became King
William I of England in 1066, following the
Battle of Hastings and the death of the Saxon
King Harold, will be familiar to many. How he
died is far less well-known.

As the Duke of Normandy as well as King of
England, William fell out with King Philip
of France in a *big* way . . . Well, William
himself must have been in a big way because
King Philip described him as looking like a
pregnant woman . . . and, for William, this
was the last straw. He was fed up with the
French regularly making incursions into his
Norman lands and failing to treat him with
the respect he felt that he deserved.

He decided to march on Paris in 1087,
stopping on the way to loot and pillage
the town of Mantes, then setting it on fire.
Unfortunately for William, his horse then trod
on a burning cinder. It reared up then came
down again, causing the king to crash up
against the pommel* of his saddle.

* The raised front part.

The result was severe internal injuries which, after six excruciatingly painful weeks, finally killed him. He was buried not in England but in his beloved Normandy.

Priest problems

Henry II (1133–89) decided that the Church, led by the Pope in Rome, had too much power and therefore in England the Church should be subject to English law, and not the other way round. Thomas à Becket, the Archbishop of Canterbury, did not agree.

Tradition has it that, in 1170, in a fit of rage,* King Henry cried out: 'Will no one rid me of this turbulent priest?', more speaking his frustration aloud than making a request** . . . but that his words were heard and four knights took it upon themselves to undertake what they took to be the king's royal decree (or, at the very least, his wishes).

Arriving in Canterbury, they found Becket at prayer in the cathedral. How it all ended was described by an eyewitness as follows:

'The wicked knight leaped suddenly upon him, cutting off the top of Becket's head. Next he received a second blow on the head, but

* From his sickbed, of all places.
** Though other versions of what he said include: 'What miserable drones and traitors have I nourished and brought up in my household, who let their lord be treated with such shameful contempt by a low-born cleric?'

362

still he stood firm and immovable. At the third blow he fell on his knees and elbows, offering himself a living sacrifice, and saying in a low voice, "For the name of Jesus and the protection of the Church, I am ready to embrace death." But the third knight inflicted a terrible wound as he lay prostrate. By this stroke, the crown of his head was separated from the head in such a way that the blood white with the brain, and the brain no less red from the blood, dyed the floor of the cathedral . . .'

The Church was horrified. Other European countries were horrified. The four knights responsible went to the Pope for forgiveness and, by way of a punishment, were each sent to fight in the Holy Lands for fourteen years.

But what could Henry do?

He walked barefoot into Canterbury and – with bleeding feet – entered the cathedral, kissing the spot where Becket was murdered. If that wasn't enough public penance – and just to be on the safe side – he had the monks, bishops and abbots line up to beat him: three strokes from each of the eighty or so monks, and five each from the others. He then spent the night in the crypt, without food or water, praying for forgiveness.

In less than three years, Becket had been made a saint, and his tomb at Canterbury soon became the most popular pilgrimage location in the country.

Fanning the flames

William the Conqueror was crowned in Westminster Abbey on Christmas Day in 1066. During the ceremony a strong guard of Norman men-at-arms and knights was posted round the abbey 'to prevent any treachery or disorder'.

When Archbishop Ealdred asked the Saxons, and Geoffrey, the Bishop of Coutances, asked the Normans if they'd accept William as their king, they shouted out with once voice – 'if not in one language' – that they would.

Unfortunately, the guards outside interpreted the loud noise of the crowd inside (along with 'the harsh accents of a foreign tongue') as a riot and – for reasons best known to them – decided the most sensible thing to do was to set fire to some buildings.

In next to no time, the fire spread from house to house and, hearing the commotion (outside this time), the crowd inside the abbey took fright and fled the coronation, leaving the archbishop, bishops and a handful of monks and clergy to finish the consecration of the trembling king.

Meanwhile, outside, some fought the flames while others took the opportunity to loot what they could in the confusion.

This wasn't quite the great start to his reign that William had been hoping for.

Famous last words

No book about kings and queens (among other people) would be complete without mentioning Queen Marie Antoinette (1755–93) and the famous line, 'Let them eat cake.' To be more accurate, the actual line translates as 'Let them eat brioche.' And, to be more accurate *still*, it seems very unlikely that Marie Antoinette ever said it.

Here's the story. During the reign of her husband, King Louis XVI, there were a number of terrible famines in France, during which thousands of poor people died of hunger. During one such famine, Marie Antoinette was told that there wasn't even any bread for them to eat, to which she replied, 'Let them eat cake,' which was rather missing the point . . .

But the story of an ignorant princess uttering such an ill-informed line appears in Jean-Jacques Rousseau's *Confessions*, which was written when Marie-Antoinette was just thirteen. In fact, it's been suggested that it was Marie Theresa of Spain who actually said it a hundred years previously. It had nothing to do with the French queen.

So why were the words put into Marie
Antoinette's mouth? Because she was queen
during the French Revolution when the people
finally rose up against their royalty and
nobility . . . and, with history being written by
the victors, this was a great way of painting
her in an even worse light, showing her to be
totally out of touch with her ordinary subjects.

Louis XVI was executed, and she followed soon after. On 16 October 1793, she was taken by open cart to the guillotine.* Her last words were, 'Pardon me, sir, I meant not to do it.' She was talking to the executioner, whose foot she'd accidentally trodden on. And no one disputes that she actually said *that*.

---

* A contraption with a huge, dropping blade, especially designed for cutting people's heads off quickly and efficiently.

PHiLip ArdaGH'S book OF

ABSOLUTELY
USELESS
LISTS

fOR aBSOLUTELY EVERY DaY Of THE YEaR

FaMOUS FictiONaL baLd FOLK, tHe
baSiC requireMeNts FOr beiNG a piRate
captaiN aNd everytHiNG yOU Never Need
to KNOW abOUT burpiNG - tHere'S a
USeLeSS LiST FOr every day OF tHe
year iN tHiS bUMper bOOk.

PHiLip ArdaGH HaS pLUNdered tHe
deepeSt cOrNerS OF HiS braiN to briNG
yOU a bOOk abOUT NotHiNG, everytHiNG
aNd SOMetHiNG eLSe eNtireLy.

PHiLiP Ardagh's bOOk OF

HOWLERS
BLUNDERS
and RANDOM
MIZTAKERY

Find out how the Pope got confused with a potato, about the footballer who ate the ref's notebook and why it's a terrible idea to get your name and date of birth tattooed on your neck in this splendid romp through the most impressive mistakes, blunders, misunderstandings, faux pas, howlers and universal truths that are not true at all!

PHENOMENAL!

The SMALL book OF BIG WORDS!

Jonathan Meres

Discover loads of big words and what they mean!

Discombobulate asinine adversaries with your verbal guile!

Fool grown-ups into thinking you're dead clever!

Work out what the heck that last sentence meant!

Become fabulously popular and successful or your money back!*

*Terms and conditions apply

Why is SNOT green?

The First Science Museum Question and Answer Book

Glenn Murphy

Why is snot green? Do rabbits fart? What is space made of? Where does all the water go at low tide? Can animals talk? What are scabs for? Will computers ever be cleverer than people?

Discover the answers to these and an awful lot of other brilliant questions frequently asked at the Science Museum in this wonderfully funny and informative book.

A selected list of titles available from Macmillan Children's Books

The prices shown below are correct at the time of going to press. However, Macmillan Publishers reserves the right to show new retail prices on covers, which may differ from those previously advertised.

All Pan Macmillan titles can be ordered from our website, www.panmacmillan.com, or from your local bookshop and are also available by post from:

Bookpost, PO Box 29, Douglas, Isle of Man IM99 1BQ

Credit cards accepted. For details:
Telephone: 01624 677237
Fax: 01624 670923
Email: bookshop@enterprise.net
www.bookpost.co.uk

Free postage and packing in the United Kingdom